MW0:613021

The Lord's Supper
AND THE BIBLE

with Scripture Passages

for

ONE HUNDRED HOMILIES

FOR THE COMMUNION SERVICE

by

Cornelius R. Stam

The Lord's Supper

AND THE BIBLE

with Scripture Passages
for
ONE HUNDRED HOMILIES
FOR THE COMMUNION SERVICE

by

Cornelius R. Stam

Founder of the *Berean Bible Society*
and
Author of over Thirty Bible Study Books,
Including the Classic Work: *Things That Differ*

BEREAN BIBLE SOCIETY
N112 W17761 Mequon Road
PO Box 756
Germantown, WI 53022
(Metro Milwaukee)

ACKNOWLEDGMENTS

The author gratefully acknowledges the help of several of his associates in preparing this volume for publication.

Heartfelt thanks go to Pastors Richard Jordan and Russell Miller, who read the manuscripts and offered many valuable suggestions.

To Pastor Ricky Kurth, also, our sincere thanks. While he labored with us at *Berean Bible Society* in 1977-1980, as our Linocomp operator, he used his "spare time" to type the author's entire *Searchlight* series on *The Lord's Supper*, most of which appears in this book without alteration.

Our beloved Chuck Milkevitch then worked with us in making the necessary changes and additions to complete the book for publication. He and Martha Kaptan also did much of the proofreading. To these "fellow laborers in the gospel" too, our sincere thanks.

CONTENTS

Contents

PREFACE

A series of articles on the Lord's Supper, written by this author, appeared in the *Berean Searchlight* in the years 1961-1963. These articles, with minor alterations and additions, are now presented to our readers in this volume.

Our purpose has not been to prepare an exhaustive exposition of all that the Bible says with regard to the Lord's Supper, but rather to consider, in the light of the Scriptures, the various doctrines which have been held and taught on this subject since the centuries when Rome held sway (called by almost common consent "the dark ages") and through the Church's emergence from this era to the present day.

In seeking the *truth* as to the Lord's Supper we must go to the Word of God alone. Here man's opinions and preferences are valueless and worse, for these are exactly what caused the confusion on the subject in the first place, and have perpetuated it in many quarters to this day. At this point a quotation from Sir Robert Anderson's book, *The Buddha of Christendom,* is germane. On Pages 61,62 of this volume he says:

"In 'all things that pertain to life and godliness' the words of Holy Writ are so simple and clear that a little child can grasp their meaning. Thus the apostle could write to Timothy, 'From a child thou hast known the Holy Scriptures, which are able to make thee wise unto salvation.' But who is to interpret the Fathers for us? Rival schools of Christian thought appeal to them in support of their opposing tenets; who, then, is to arbitrate between them? And by what standard? And why should we turn from what is plain and simple to writings which are a maze of mingled heresy and truth?"

The following consideration of man's hopelessly confused teachings as to the Lord's Supper, in the light of *what God says* on the subject will, we believe, bring out the truth as to what, essentially, the Lord's Supper *is* and how it should be celebrated.

It is our fervent prayer that this volume will give the reader a clear and satisfying understanding of what the Scriptures, "rightly divided," teach as to the Lord's Supper, and will serve to make his every participation in this touching memorial a truly blessed experience.

CORNELIUS R. STAM

Chicago, Illinois
June 15, 1981

INTRODUCTION

"For I have received of the Lord that which also I delivered unto you, That the Lord Jesus, the same night in which He was betrayed, took bread:

"And when He had given thanks, He brake it, and said, Take, eat; this is My body, which is broken for you: this do in remembrance of Me.

"After the same manner also He took the cup, when He had supped, saying, This cup is the new testament in My blood: this do ye, as oft as ye drink it, in remembrance of Me.

"For as often as ye eat this bread, and drink this cup, ye do show the Lord's death till He come."

—I Cor. 11:23-26

The questions surrounding the commemoration of the Lord's Supper are many and varied, and among the millions who observe it there are deep doctrinal divisions.

The Roman Catholic Church, for example, teaches that upon their consecration by the priest, the bread and wine are changed into the actual body and blood of Christ; that the Sacrifice of the Mass (as she calls the Lord's Supper) is a sacramental renewal, again and again, of the sacrifice of our Lord's body and blood on Calvary's cross; that He is actually immolated, or slain, in every Sacrifice of the Mass and that this sacrifice avails as a satisfaction to God for sin.

Martin Luther denounced all this, but taught, as the Lutheran Church still does, that while in the "sacra-

xiii

ment" of the Lord's Supper the substances of the bread and wine remain, the substances of Christ's body and blood are united with them. [1] Further, while denying that the Lord's Supper is a *sacrifice* for sins (on the basis of Heb. 10:14,18) the Lutheran Church, with Luther, teaches that "in the sacrament forgiveness of sins, life, and salvation are given us" through Christ's words: "Given and shed for you for the remission of sins."

John Calvin, father of the Reformed and Presbyterian Churches, in turn denied both transubstantiation and consubstantiation, but taught that "Christ bestows upon the faithful receiver of the sacrament, not, indeed, the substance, but the saving power of His body . . .all the benefits which Christ, by His body, has procured for us."

Ulrich Zwingli, unlike them all, held that the word "is" (in "this *is* My body . . .My blood") simply means *signifies* and that the bread and wine are merely symbols of Christ's body and blood, offered in sacrifice for us, and are therefore to be partaken of as such, in grateful *memory* of His death for our sins.

The Plymouth Brethren hold that the Lord's Supper is a *memorial* of the death of Christ for us but, on the basis of Acts 2:42, 20:7, *et al*, they call it "the breaking of bread" and teach that this memorial should be observed faithfully *every* Sunday (which they call "The Lord's Day.")

The Friends, or Quakers, and the Salvation Army

---

1. The Roman Catholic view is called *transubstantiation*; the Lutheran, *consubstantiation*.

deny that a *physical* remembrance of the Lord's death is included in God's plan for the members of the Body of Christ, as do some who, we feel, go to dispensational extremes.

A great multitude of believers, in and out of the recognized denominations, look upon the Lord's Supper as simply a *memorial* of Christ's death for us, believing without qualification in the *finished* and *all-sufficient* redemption wrought by Christ on Calvary.

Even among these there have been questions as to mode, method and frequency of observance, but there is a more basic question still which is dispensational in character, i.e., whether the Supper should be observed at all during the present dispensation of "the mystery."

It is our purpose to deal with these views at some length and to determine from the Word, rightly divided, just what should be our faith and practice with regard to the Lord's Supper.

Chapter I

The Church of Rome
and the Sacrifice of the Mass

We have before us a copy of the *Saint Joseph Daily Missal*, published under the copyright of the *Catholic Book Publishing Co.*, of N.Y. (1959) and bearing the imprimatur of *Francis Cardinal Spellman.* This missal instructs Roman Catholics as to the meaning of "Holy Mass" and how it should be celebrated.

At hand, too, we have a copy of *The Question Box*, by a Paulist Father, *Bertrand L. Conway*, published by the *Paulist Press*, of N.Y. (1960) and bearing the imprimatur of *Patrick Cardinal Hayes.* Also, two editions of *A Catholic Dictionary*, one published by the *Catholic Publication Society, Co.* (1884) bearing the imprimatur of *John Cardinal McCloskey* and another, published years later by the *MacMillan Company* (1958) and bearing the imprimatur of two Catholic prelates: *E. Morrogh Bernard* and *Georgius L. Craven.* [1]

Finally, before us are two Roman Catholic translations of the Scriptures: the old *Douay Version* and the *Confraternity Revision* of the New Testament. [2]

From these and other official sources we will quote pertinent passages as we examine the Roman Catholic doctrine of the Mass.

---

1. We will identify these, respectively: (Cath. Publ. Soc.) and (MacMillan Co.).

2. Herein identified as (*D.V.*) and (*C.R.*).

THE DOCTRINE OF TRANSUBSTANTIATION

On Page 6 of the *St. Joseph Daily Missal* it is stated that "In the name of the Whole Church, the priest offers to God the bread and wine, mixed with a few drops of water, which will be *changed into the Body and Blood of Christ*" (Our ital.). Again, on Page 7, it declares that "Speaking through the priest our Blessed Lord changes the bread and wine into His own Body and Blood, Soul and Divinity."

The *Catholic Dictionary* (Cath. Publ. Soc.) states that upon consecration by the priest "The substance of bread and wine ceases to be, for it is changed into Christ's body and blood."

This doctrine is called the "Real Presence," i.e., of Christ, in what *appears* to be bread and wine.

Prior to 1215 A.D., Roman Catholics could accept or reject this doctrine, but after that date they dare not deny it upon pain of everlasting punishment. Why it became so important at so late a date or why an ordinance of saving value was not proclaimed by "the Church" as one of its cardinal tenets until the year 1215 are questions Rome has never satisfactorily answered.

Today, not only Roman Catholics, but *all* of us are informed that we *must* believe this doctrine or perish. At the thirteenth session of the *Council of Trent* (Oct., 1551) "the Church" pronounced a curse upon those who deny the doctrine of the Real Presence.

Referring to "that wonderful and singular conversion of the whole substance of the bread into the body, and of the wine into the blood, the appearances of the

17

bread and wine alone remaining," the council declared:
"If any one shall deny that the body and blood, together
with the soul and Divinity of our Lord Jesus Christ,
and therefore the whole Christ, are truly, really and
substantially contained in the Sacrament of the Holy
Eucharist, let him be anathema" (Conc. Trid., Sess. 13,
de Euchar, can. 1.).

Thus we *must* believe what is contrary to our
God-given reason or be *anathema—accursed.*

The Church of Rome has never rescinded this action
but has emphasized it again and again through her
popes. Nor did *Vatican II* change any of this, as an
examination of the *Conciliar and Post Conciliar Documents* will reveal.

TRUTH OR SUPERSTITION?

Despite all Rome's efforts to make this doctrine
sound reasonable, at least to faith, it still remains an
outstanding example of the sheer superstition with
which Catholic doctrine and practice are so replete.

The priest's consecration of the bread and wine
clearly effect no physical change in them. They still
look like bread and wine, *taste* like bread and wine and,
chemically analyzed, would be pronounced bread and
wine. Yet Rome insists that they are no longer bread
and wine, but the *actual substance* of the *body* and
blood of Christ, together with His soul and divinity—
the *whole* Christ, to be "immolated," or slain, again in
a renewal of the sacrifice of Calvary. And we are told
that we *must* believe this or be cursed by "the Church."

But did not our Lord work many miracles? Yes, but
where among them all do we find even one that was

contrary to reason and nature? God still works miracles every day (though not as prophetic "signs") as He turns grass into milk and meat, etc., but all His miracles are *super*natural; none are *contra*natural.

But did not our Lord turn water into wine? Yes, He did, and when He had done so it *was* wine and *tasted* like it, as the "governor," or "chief steward" of the feast testified (John 2:9,10).

But if turning bread and wine into flesh and blood—which still looks, feels and tastes like bread and wine—is contrary to reason, imagine the strain on our God-given intelligence when we are asked to believe that our Lord, at that first Lord's Supper, while still standing there in the flesh, actually turned the bread and wine into His own flesh and blood, so that with His own hands, He presented to them His body and blood! This is what Rome teaches, on the basis of the words: *"This is My body...My blood."*

In seeking to explain this Rome has always been embarrassed by multiplied absurdities, not the least of which is the direct implication that the actual body and blood of our Lord Jesus Christ are 1.) swallowed and digested in the stomachs 2.) of millions of people at the same time, 3.) scattered over wide areas, and 4.) some of them, at least, insincere and impious.

To those who will reasonably consider any segment of the above implication the observance of the Mass *must* appear a monstrous absurdity of superstition rather than an act of intelligent faith.

We will deal with our Lord's words at the Supper later, but here we point out only that the so-called

19

"miracle" of the Mass is unlike *any* miracle of Scripture. It is not merely above human reason; it is *contrary* to it, so that the "consecration" by the priest assumes the character of a magical incantation rather than a spiritual consecration.

Rome would ask us to believe her, to exercise a blind "faith" which is nothing more than superstition, but as we turn to the Word of God we find that *He* accepts only intelligent faith. [3] Hear the Apostle Paul declare:

"I will pray with the spirit, and *I will pray with the understanding also*: I will sing with the spirit, and *I will sing with the understanding also*" (I Cor. 14:15).

And hear his earnest prayer for believers:

"That the God of our Lord Jesus Christ, the Father of glory, may give unto you the spirit of *wisdom* and *revelation*, in the *knowledge* of Him: the eyes of your *understanding* being enlightened . . ." (Eph. 1:17,18).

"That ye might be filled with *the knowledge of His will* in all *wisdom and spiritual understanding*" *(Col. 1:9)*.

Witness the Apostle's "great conflict" for the saints, that they might enjoy:

" . . .*the full assurance of understanding*" (Col. 2:2).

THE SCRIPTURES INVOLVED

But did not our Lord say: *"This is My body . . . .This is My blood"?*

Rome insists that these words of our Lord, recorded in the synoptic "gospels," must be *literally* interpreted.

---

3. See the author's booklet: *Your Faith in God's Word, Is It Superstitious or Intelligent?*

Our Lord said: "This *is* My body" and "this *is* My blood," so, upon their consecration by the priest, they *are* just that.

Now this is passing strange, for there is probably no segment of the professing Church whose theologians so often object to literal interpretations. Read the footnotes in both the *Douay* and *Confraternity* editions of the Bible and see how often they *explain away* what the Scriptures actually say. Yet, in this case they will not permit even the most natural symbolic rendering.

In our Lord's parables of the kingdom of heaven, He said: "The field *is* the world . . . .the enemy . . .*is* the devil . . . .the harvest *is* the end of the world and the reapers *are* the angels" (Matt. 13:38,39; *C.R.*). St. Paul likewise declares that "Mount Sinai . . .*is* Agar" (Gal. 4:25; *C.R.*) and that "the rock [4] *was* Christ" (I Cor. 10:4; *C.R.*). The word "is" in each of these cases clearly signifies *represents*; the former *represents* the latter. But this natural interpretation cannot be allowed with regard to our Lord's words about the bread and the cup!

Why not? The *Question Box* answers: "These texts [above] are parallel to one another, but not to the words of the institution . . . .They are not even grammatically parallel, because with one exception they all have for their subject a noun, whereas the words of the institution have as their subject a demonstrative adverb."

This is interesting, for we had always considered the

---

4. From which the children of Israel drank in the wilderness.

word "this" to be a pronoun [5] referring in this case to the bread and the wine. Indeed, in each record of this incident it is clearly stated that our Lord *took the bread and the wine* and said: *"This* is" etc.

The interesting fact is that this makes Rome's interpretation *self*-contradictory. In Matt. 26:26 we read that "Jesus took *bread* and said, 'Take and eat; *this* is My body.' " What did He take into His hands? *"Bread."* And it was this *bread* which He gave them to eat, saying: "This is My body." Had He said: "This *has now become* My body," we might accept the doctrine of transubstantiation but, according to Rome's own insistence that "is" means *"is,"* we conclude that it was *the bread* which He called His body, i.e., *as representing it.*

If this is not the correct interpretation of His words, then what about Luke's fuller record, where the Lord says: "This cup *is* the new covenant in My blood"? (Luke 22:20; I Cor. 11:25; *C.R.*). Perhaps sacerdotalists will explain how a *cup* can become a *covenant.* The Roman Catholic translations have no footnote to explain this. Obviously the cup and its contents *represented* the new covenant.

Another important fact in this connection is that in the Greek (and Hebrew) the substantive *to be* is *not expressed* when dealing with simple matters of fact. Thus in the *Authorized* rendering of II Tim. 3:16, "All Scripture is given by inspiration of God," the "is" appears in italics. This indicates that the word was *supplied* [6] by the translators and is *not found in the*

---

5. A word used in the place of a noun.

6. Correctly so, for the English requires it to render the true sense.

22

original. But when a symbol or figure of speech is intended, the word "is" must be used. Thus in the phrases: "The field *is* the world," etc., the word "is" *does* appear in the Greek. Its appearance in our Lord's words about the bread and cup, therefore, indicate that He was using a figure of speech; that the bread and wine *represented* His body and blood.

It is most evident that the twelve interpreted His words so, for, with all the questions already filling their minds about Christ and His death, how could they have been so ready to believe something so grotesque and utterly contrary to all reason, as that Christ, Himself sitting at the table before their eyes, yet offered them His own body and blood to eat and drink? By eating and drinking without hesitation they testified that *they* understood Christ's words as we do, i.e., that the bread and wine *represented* His body and blood. And mark well, they *ate and drank*; they did not *adore* the elements.

The Apostle Paul says of the Israelites in the wilderness that they *"all ate the same spiritual food, and all drank the same spiritual drink (for they drank from the spiritual rock which followed them, and the rock was Christ)"* (I Cor. 10:3,4; *C.R.*).

This, of course, means that the rock *became* (or should have become) *thus significant to them*, for it was that water which also quenched their physical thirst. This is not transubstantiation but the translation of physical blessings into spiritual ones. One can easily understand, for example, how Isaac became a great spiritual blessing to Abraham after he had offered him to God in sacrifice.

Thus the Apostle declares:

"The *cup* of blessing which we bless, is it not the *communion* of the blood of Christ? The *bread* which we break, is it not the *communion* [7] of the body of Christ?" (I Cor. 10:16).

Mark well, he does not say that the cup and bread *are* the blood and body of Christ, but that they are the *communion* of His blood and body. I.e., believers worship God together as they meditate on the fact that His body was broken, and His blood shed, *for them.*

---

7. We regret that both Roman Catholic versions have rendered the word *koinonia* "partaking" in the latter part of the verse only. It is the same word "communion" in both cases. It is theirs to explain why they rendered this same word in two different ways in one verse.

Chapter II

"An Hard Saying"

"Then Jesus said unto them, Verily, verily, I say unto you, Except ye eat the flesh of the Son of man, and drink His blood, ye have no life in you.

"Whoso eateth My flesh, and drinketh My blood, hath eternal life; and I will raise him up at the last day" (John 6:53,54).

In His discourse on the bread of life our Lord does not mention the Lord's Supper, nor does the above passage have any reference whatever to it, but in Rome's theology it is used as one of the strongest arguments for transubstantiation and on the basis of these words we are asked, yea commanded, to believe that our Lord actually meant defiled and sinful human beings to physically *eat His flesh* and *drink His blood.* And we must take part in a superstition so horrible and repulsive to obtain everlasting life!

Let us then examine the passage at length.

Our Lord had called Himself *"the living bread which came down from heaven"* and had added: *"The bread that I will give, is My flesh, for the life of the world"* (John 6:51,52; *D.V.*).

When the Jews strove among themselves and asked: *"How can this man give us His flesh to eat?"* He did not modify or qualify His statement but insisted that if they did not partake of His flesh and blood they had no life in them and that everlasting life depended upon their thus partaking (John 6:53,55).

25

Did our Lord say that it was at the Lord's Supper, or the Mass, that they should *repeatedly* eat and drink His flesh and blood? In no wise. And did He mean that they should *physically* partake of His flesh and blood? Evidently not, for He contrasted this "bread from heaven" with the manna in the wilderness, that other "bread from heaven," of which the Israelites partook physically, only to die again (Ver. 49; *D.V.*). Indeed, as early as Verse 27 we hear Him say: *"Do not labor for the food that perishes, but for that which endures unto life everlasting."* And certainly He stressed the *difference* between physical food and Himself as "the bread from heaven" when He said: "My flesh is meat *indeed*: and My blood is drink *indeed*" (Ver. 56; *D.V.*). Then, when He insisted that they should partake of His flesh and blood and His own disciples said: *"This is an hard saying,"* our Lord explained:

"It is the spirit that quickeneth [giveth life]: the flesh profiteth nothing. The words that I have spoken to you, are spirit and life" (Ver. 64; D.V.).

And if this be not enough, we have our Lord's clear declaration, in this same passage, with regard to this same subject, explaining what it is to "eat His flesh and drink His blood."

"I am the bread of life: he that cometh to Me shall not hunger: and he that believeth in Me shall never thirst" (Ver. 35; D.V.).

"And this is the will of the Father that sent Me: that every one who seeth the Son and believeth in Him, may have life everlasting, and I will raise him up in the last day" (Ver. 40; D.V.).

Our Lord often used food and drink in figures of speech. To those who had brought Him food on another occasion, and were urging Him to partake, He said: *"I have food to eat of which you do not know"* (John 4:33; *C.R.*) and *"My food is to do the will of Him who sent Me"* (Ver. 34).

The reason His flesh and blood are emphasized in John 6:53,54 is because He *"*bore our sins *in His own body* on the tree" (I Pet. 2:24; *D.V.*) and gave His life for us, that we might have it.

As we accept His finished work by faith we *partake*, as it were, of His flesh and blood and receive the life He gave for us.

In other words, the life we receive from Him does not consist of the mere *knowledge* of what He has done for us, but of *partaking* of Him; not in seeing the table spread, but in *partaking* of the food.

Thus by the work of the Holy Spirit, the believer truly becomes one with Christ. Unless this is so no analogy can be taken from being fed by food and drink.

IDOLATRY

But the Sacrifice of the Mass is worse than superstition; it is *idolatry*, for the bread and the cup are "elevated" at the Mass, for the worshippers *"to see and adore."*

Rome, of course, objects that the worshippers do not adore the apparent physical object, but only the Christ concealed beneath it. But we answer that this is the very essence of idolatry. Even the pagans in heathen lands protest that they do not actually worship that stone or that tree but only the spirit concealed invisibly behind it or represented by it. But to worship God

27

under any physical appearance is idolatry. Thus we read in the Law:

"Thou shalt not make unto thee any graven image, or any likeness of anything that is in heaven above, or that is in the earth beneath, or that is in the water under the earth.

"Thou shalt not bow down thyself to them, nor serve [worship] them . . ." (Ex. 20:4,5).

Heathenism did not begin with the worship of other gods, but with the *corruption* of the worship of the *true* God, as they made images to represent *Him*. Thus Rom. 1:20-23 declares:

" . . . they are without excuse:

"Because that, when they knew God, they glorified Him not as God . . . but . . . changed the glory of the incorruptible God into an image made like to corruptible man, and to birds, and four-footed beasts, and creeping things."

In the case of Rome the Lord Jesus Christ, God the Son, is supposed to be concealed in a wafer and some wine which are "elevated" with solemn ceremony for the people to "see and adore."

INCONSISTENCIES, CONTRADICTIONS AND DOUBLE TALK

To explain all this "the Church" has involved herself in gross inconsistencies, contradictions and double talk.

TRANSUBSTANTIATION AND CONCOMITANCE

The *Catholic Dictionary* (MacMillan Co.) under the word *Transubstantiation* states:

28

"The word is defined by the Council of Trent as 'the wonderful and singular conversion of the whole substance of the bread into the Body of Christ and of the whole substance of the wine into the Blood...' (Sess. XIII, Can. 2)."

Mark this definition well. The *bread* is changed into Christ's *body* and the *wine* into His *blood*.

But if we must partake of His flesh and blood to gain eternal life, why does "the Church" deny the cup to the laity?

This is explained in the same *Catholic Dictionary* under the word *Concomitance*, where it is declared that *both* the body and blood are present under the "species," or appearance, of *both* the bread and the wine.

But we thought the *bread* was changed into the *body* and the *wine* into the *blood* of Christ!

The same double talk is used to "explain" this difficulty on pages 255 and 259 of the *Question Box*.

The Scriptures, anticipating this very error, records *only* with regard to the *cup*, our Lord's words: *"ALL of you drink of this"* (Matt. 26:27; *C.R.*).

Rome, of course, argues that our Lord instructed His disciples to partake of the Lord's Supper only as His priests and representatives, but in that case why *do* they serve the host (the bread) to the laity? Clearly, if the laity are to partake at all, they are *all* to *drink* [1] of the cup. If they are *not* to partake, they should *not* eat

---

1. The doctrine of concomitance fails here, for one cannot *drink* a wafer. Thus Rome denies the cup to the laity while insisting that men must *drink* Christ's blood to receive eternal life!

the host. Yet Rome allows the laity to partake of the host but denies them the cup!

THE "UNBLOODY" SACRIFICE

The Sacrifice of the Mass is called the "unbloody" sacrifice of the Body of the living Christ, yet He is said to be "immolated" (slain in sacrifice) on Catholic altars. How can this be? How could His actual body be slain in sacrifice without the shedding of blood?

Further, if the Mass is an "unbloody" sacrifice, how can it avail as a satisfaction to God for sin, as Rome claims?

When God provided animal sacrifices for the people of Israel, He said:

"For the life of the flesh is in the blood: and I have given it to you upon the altar to make an atonement for your souls: for it is the blood that maketh an atonement for the soul" (Lev. 17:11).

And some fifteen hundred years later Paul declared by divine inspiration:

"Without shedding of blood is no remission" (Heb. 9:22).

We shall see more such inconsistencies, contradictions and double talk when we examine Rome's teachings and claims regarding her priesthood.

Chapter III

The Altar, The Camp
and The Priesthood

"We have an altar, whereof they have no right to eat which serve the tabernacle.

"For the bodies of those beasts, whose blood is brought into the sanctuary by the high priest for sin, are burned without the camp.

"Wherefore Jesus also, that He might sanctify the people with His own blood, suffered without the gate.

"Let us go forth therefore unto Him, without [outside] the camp, bearing His reproach."

—Heb. 13:10-13

THE BELIEVER'S ALTAR

Under the word "altar," the *Catholic Dictionary* (MacMillan Co.) reads as follows:

"An altar is that upon which sacrifice is offered. The Christian Sacrifice of the Mass, though not necessarily offered in a church or chapel, must always be offered on an altar, or an altar stone . . . which is, in fact, a very small portable altar, and is sometimes so called. An altar or altar stone must contain relics and be consecrated by a bishop or by a prelate having the faculties."

Thus the Church of Rome has erected an altar—indeed, thousands of altars—for the sacrifice of the body and blood of Christ in the Mass. Many of her

31

individual churches, even, have more than one altar, the principal one being called the "high altar" or the "main altar."

This, though an earlier *Catholic Dictionary* (Cath. Publ. Soc.) states, under the same word: "Whether the Christian altar is mentioned by name in the Bible is doubtful."

There is, of course, no mention of a physical Christian altar in the Bible, and the above passage from Hebrews 13, though used by many a Catholic theologian in defense of the Mass, cannot possibly have any relation to it.

The Lord's Supper is never associated with an *altar* in Scripture. On the contrary, the Apostle Paul, by inspiration of the Spirit, draws a *contrast* here between the altars of the Old Testament and the cross of Christ, between type and antitype, between shadow and substance.

His reference in this passage is, of course, to the "sin offering," offered on the annual Day of Atonement—an offering of which neither the priesthood nor the offerer was permitted to partake. Why not? Because more than any other, it spoke of an *un*finished work. But now, through Christ, the work of redemption has been gloriously accomplished and we may all joyfully partake of the fruits.

Therefore, says the Apostle, *"We have an altar, whereof they have no right to eat which [still] serve the tabernacle"* (Ver. 10) for they are still occupied with the types, the shadows.

32

The altar whereof we partake is an appreciation of Christ Himself, and the sacrifices we offer are spiritual rather than physical. This is clear from the context. In the preceding verse (Ver. 9) the Apostle declares: *"For it is a good thing that the heart be established with grace; not with meats, which have not profited them that have been occupied therein,"* while in Verse 15 he concludes:

"By Him therefore let us offer the sacrifice of praise to God continually, that is, the fruit of our lips, giving thanks to His name."

Thus does the Apostle, by divine inspiration, contrast the altars of Judaism with that spiritual altar whereon believers today offer the sacrifice of praise and partake of the blessings of the finished work of Christ. How, then, can we countenance the thousands of altars of Rome, on which the actual body and blood of Christ are said to be offered again and again in the Mass as an atonement for sin?

OUTSIDE THE CAMP

Verse 11, of the passage we are here considering, reminds us that the carcass of the sin offering, on the annual Day of Atonement, was burned "without," or *outside* "the camp," i.e., the camp of Israel, and the significance of this is immediately pointed out:

"Wherefore Jesus also, that He might sanctify the people with His own blood, suffered without the gate" (Ver. 12).

The Lord Jesus suffered "without the camp," rejected by His own. This is why the Apostle now exhorts us:

33

"Let us go forth therefore unto Him, without the camp, bearing His reproach" (Ver. 13).

Mark well, he does not say: "Let us go forth from the camp of Israel to another camp—the Church." No, neither these Jewish believers nor we are exhorted to go from one camp to another. We are rather exhorted to "go forth...*unto Him, without the camp.*" The *true* Church is not an organization but *a living organism*, the Body of Christ, who *alone* is its Head. Surely the professing Church has not borne witness to this fact as it has divided itself into hundreds of mutually exclusive camps. The true believer, being joined to Christ the Head, belongs to *all* other true believers. This, even though *they* have separated themselves from Him by forming or joining "camps" of their own.

Above all others the Church of Rome has set herself up as a "camp" to which man must "belong." And worse, she has reared thousands upon thousands of altars at which her priests presume to offer again and again the actual body and blood of Christ in the Sacrifice of the Mass, as though He had not completed the work of redemption on Calvary's cross.

OUR GREAT HIGH PRIEST

The *Catholic Dictionary* (Cath. Publ. Soc.) states, under "Priests, Christian": "The words 'priest,' 'priesthood'...are never applied in the New Testament to the office of the Christian ministry. All Christians are said to be priests (I Pet. 2:5,9; Apoc. 5:10). This recognition of the universal priesthood of Christians, however, involves no denial of the existence of a special priesthood, for the Israelites too were called a 'kingdom

of priests,' though they had, of course, a special priesthood with prerogatives jealously guarded." Under the
same heading it is stated that the priest "succeeds the
Jewish 'elder' as well as the Jewish priest."

But if, as this *Catholic Dictionary* states: "The words
'priest,' 'priesthood' are never applied in the New
Testament to the office of the Christian ministry," on
what basis does Rome operate her elaborate priesthood? Certainly not on the authority of the Word of
God. If a priesthood is in God's plan for the Church of
this dispensation, why is the word "priest" never
applied either to the twelve apostles or to Paul and his
associates in the ministry, Barnabas, Silas, Timothy,
Titus, *et al?* This surely *does* involve a denial of any
special priesthood today. The priests of Old Testament times were so called, and the mere fact that there
was an organized priesthood *then* by no means proves
that there should be an organized priesthood *now.*

Nowhere in Scripture—even in the Roman Catholic
translation—is it indicated that the Catholic priest
"succeeds...the Jewish priest." This is a pure inven-
tion of an apostate "Church" which does not recognize
the all-sufficiency of our Lord's accomplished redemption or the final authority of the Word of God.

Further, the *Catholic Dictionary* is certainly in error
when it states that "the Israelites...were called a
'kingdom of priests,' " for their own *Douay* translation
of Ex. 19:5,6 records God's challenge to Israel at the
giving of the Ten Commandments:

> *"If therefore you will hear My voice, and keep My covenant . . .
> you shall be to Me a priestly kingdom, and a holy nation."*

Did Israel keep God's covenant, the Law? Indeed not. They broke its very first commandment before Moses even got down from Mt. Sinai and they continued to break it ever after, with the result that Israel did not, and has not yet, become "a kingdom of priests." It is precisely because of this failure on Israel's part that Christ died for them on Calvary, shedding the blood of the *New* Covenant, that *by grace* they might still become "a royal priesthood." This is what Peter refers to in writing to the Jewish dispersion in I Pet. 2:5,9 and its full realization for Israel is still future.

The *Catholic Catechism* (P. 189) states that "The dignity of the priesthood is very great . . .he is a mediator between God and man, with power over the real as well as the mystical Body of Christ." Thus too, Cardinal H. E. Manning, in the *Eternal Priesthood* (P. 12, Burns, 1883) declared that the priest has "jurisdiction over the natural and over the mystical Body of Christ."

Imagine any poor mortal having "power" or "jurisdiction" over the "real" or "natural" body of *Christ, the Son of God!* Even in the days of His humiliation He said with regard to His life:

"No one takes it from Me, but I lay it down of Myself. I have the power to lay it down, and I have the power to take it up again" (John 10:18; C.R.).

Yet Roman priests presume to bring Him down from heaven at will to "immolate," or slay Him again and again in their sacrifices.

But if this be contrary to Holy Scripture, fully as contrary is the teaching that the priest has "power" or "jurisdiction" over the *"mystical"* Body, i.e., to grant or deny her communicants absolution from sin.

Think of the presumption that would lead any priest to call himself "a mediator between God and man," when his own Bible declares:

"For there is one God, and one mediator between God and men, Himself man, Christ Jesus, who gave Himself a ransom for all..." (I Tim. 2:5,6; C.R.).

Consider the blasphemy of recognizing tens of thousands of such "mediators" when God declares that there is *one* and *only one*, our Lord Jesus Christ!

The Roman Catholic versions of the New Testament declare, not once, but again and again, and emphasize in varied phraseology, that there is no "special priesthood" today but only *one* divine Priest, *"a Priest forever, after the order of Melchisedec."* Let us be Bereans and see whether these things are so:

Melchisedec, "king of Salem, priest of the most high God," was a type of Christ, our divine High Priest, in that he was "without father, without mother, without genealogy, having neither beginning of days nor end of life" as far as the Genesis record goes (See Heb. 7:1-3; *C.R.*).

Now, David prophesied of Christ, about a thousand years before His coming:

"The Lord hath sworn, and will not repent, Thou art a priest for ever after the order of Melchisedec" (Psa. 110:4).

The Apostle Paul argues from this that the appointment of Christ as a High Priest of another order signifies the failure and passing away of the Levitical priesthood:

"If then perfection was by the Levitical priesthood (for under it the people received the Law), what further need was there that another priest should rise, according to the order of Melchisedech . . .?" (Heb. 7:11; C.R.).

Declaring in the next verse that "the priesthood is changed," the Apostle presses his argument that the "many priests" of Old Testament times were superseded by *one* great Priest, the Lord Jesus Christ. Referring to the Levitical priests, he says:

"And the other priests indeed were numerous, because they were prevented by death from continuing in office, but He [*Christ*], *because He continues forever, has an everlasting priesthood.* Therefore He is able at all times to save those who come to God through Him, since He lives always to make intercession for them" (Heb. 7:23-25; C.R.).

From this passage it is evident that the "numerous" priests of the Old Testament have been replaced by the *one* great Priest who "continues forever." Indeed, he goes on to say, in the next chapter:

"Now *the main point* in what we are saying is this. We have such a *high priest, who has taken His seat at the right hand of the throne of majesty in the heavens, a minister of the holies, and of the true tabernacle, which the Lord has erected and not man*" (Heb. 8:1,2; C.R.).

And continuing his comparison of our Lord's priesthood with that of the many priests of old, he says:

"But now He has obtained *a superior ministry*, in proportion as He is Mediator of *a superior covenant*, enacted on the basis of

38

superior promises. For had the first been faultless, place would not, of course, be sought for the second" (Vers. 6,7: C.R.).

In Chapter 10, still pursuing the same important theme, the Apostle points out, perhaps most clearly of all, the full competency of our *one* great Priest:

"And every priest indeed stands daily ministering, and often offering the same sacrifices, which can never take away sins; but Jesus, having offered one sacrifice for sins, has taken His seat forever at the right hand of God . . . .For by one offering He has perfected forever those who are sanctified" (Heb. 10:11-14; C.R.).

In the light of this do we now need human priests to grant us absolution from our sins and bring us near to God? The Apostle himself gives us the answer:

"Since then, brethren, we are free to enter the holies in virtue of the blood of Christ, a new and living way which He inaugurated for us through the veil (that is, His flesh), and since we have a high priest over the house of God, let us draw near. . ." (Vers. 19-22; C.R.).

How the Roman Catholic Bible itself annihilates the very idea of any priest outside of Christ in this dispensation of grace! Not only are "the words 'priest,' 'priesthood' never applied in the New Testament to the office of the Christian ministry," as the *Catholic Dictionary* says, but the epistles of Paul, and especially that to the Hebrews, unreservedly condemn the formation of a priesthood in the present dispensation of grace.

What a contrast between the glad memorial of Christ's finished and all-sufficient work on Calvary, which the Apostle Paul outlines for us in I Cor.

11:23-26, and the supposed sacrifice again and again of the actual body and blood of Christ by a human priest in the Mass in order to make atonement for sin!

Chapter IV

One All-Sufficient Sacrifice

The gravest heresy of the Church of Rome is doubtless her doctrine of the "perpetual sacrifice," the offering of the body and blood of our Lord on altars in endless repetition by her priests. Her many sacrifices, like her many priests, constitute a repudiation of the plainest Scriptures—in her own translations of the Bible—and cast reflections upon the all-sufficiency of the redemptive work of Christ on Calvary.

ROME'S "PERPETUAL SACRIFICE"
CHRIST A VICTIM

Let us see what the Church of Rome has to say about her "perpetuation" of Christ's sacrifice on the cross and then, like the Bereans of old, let us search the Scriptures to see for ourselves whether these things are so.

First, Rome teaches that in each Mass our Lord Jesus Christ is brought down from heaven by the priest and that, "subjecting Himself" to the "jurisdiction" of the priest as a "victim," He is "immolated," or slain, the priest offering Him to God in sacrifice for sin.

The Maryknoll Missal (P. J. Kennedy and Sons, N.Y.) states: "The Sacrifice of the altar is no mere commemoration of the Sacrifice of the Cross. It is one and the same Victim....our divine Redeemer in His human nature with His true body and blood....Thus the Sacrifice of Calvary is repeated in every sacrifice of the altar" (P. XVII).

41

The *Saint Joseph Daily Missal* (J. P. Daleiden Co., Chicago) says: "Christ our Head is the priest and the victim of every Mass" (P. 3). He "becomes really present" and "in a state of victimhood" (P. 3).

Cardinal H. E. Manning, in writing of the sacrifice of Christ in the Mass, declared: "In this divine manner He subjects Himself to the jurisdiction of His priests..." (*Eternal Priesthood*, Burns, 1883, P. 12).

The Faith of Millions, by J. A. O'Brien, states: "...the Mass perpetuates the sacrifice of the Cross by offering to God the same Victim that was immolated on Calvary for the redemption of man" (P. 366).

Instructions for Non-Catholics adds to this: "The Mass today is the same as the Last Supper. The priest at Mass brings down upon the altar our Lord Jesus Christ, offers Him to God for our sins, and gives Him to the people in Holy Communion" (P. 7).

From the above it should already be evident that Roman Catholic declarations as to our Lord's accomplished redemption cannot be taken at their face value, but as if to emphasize this fact, Catholic writers actually contend that His death at Calvary alone did *not* make complete satisfaction to God for sin.

The Catholic Church From Within: "In vain would our Lord have...died for us on the cross, if He had not left us this Blessed Memorial of His Passion" (P. 170).

"One Mass," says an advertisement of *Saint Joseph Daily Missal*, "makes more atonement for sin and pleads more eloquently than does the combined worship of all the souls in heaven, on earth and in purgatory."

There should be no misunderstanding on this point then. Rome teaches that the sacramental "renewal of Christ's sacrifice" is efficacious as a satisfaction to God for sin, and that without it our Lord would have died in vain. This can mean nothing but that the sacrifice of Christ at Calvary was *not fully* efficacious.

The Church of Rome, then, teaches:

1. That "the Sacrifice of Calvary is repeated in every Sacrifice of the altar."

2. That at each Mass our Lord "subjects Himself" to the "jurisdiction" of the priest.

3. That at each Mass He again becomes a Victim.

4. That the priest offers him to God as a satisfaction for sin, immolated, or slain, on the altar "in His human nature, with His true body and blood."

This is how Rome has interpreted and enlarged upon the Scriptures which deal with the Lord's Supper, the memorial of His death for sinners.

CHRIST THE VICTOR

In subjecting all this to the light of the Word of God itself, it should perhaps be noted first that our Lord is no longer to be considered a victim—not even in His death at Calvary.

It is true that Isaiah 53 and other Old Testament prophecies depict Him as a sacrificial victim, as a lamb led to the slaughter. It is true too, that through Pentecost He was still looked upon in this light; that the crucifixion was viewed, not as something He had wrought, but as something He had allowed others to do to Him. Thus the Apostle Peter, at Pentecost and just after, hurled this charge at his hearers:

"Him, being delivered by the determinate counsel and fore-knowledge of God, ye have taken, and by wicked hands have crucified and slain" (Acts 2:23).

"Ye denied the Holy One and the Just, and desired a murderer to be granted unto you;

"And killed the Prince of life . . ." (Acts 3:14,15).

But with the raising up of Paul, a new light was shed on the crucifixion of Christ. To him was committed "the secret of the gospel," which was the essence of his "preaching of the cross." In his epistles our Lord is seen, not as the Victim but as the *Victor* at Calvary. The death of the cross is no longer seen merely as something that He *suffered*, but as something that He *accomplished*. For example, it is written:

"Who, being the brightness of His [God's] glory and the image of His substance, and upholding all things by the word of His power, *has effected man's purgation from sin and taken His seat at the right hand of the majesty on high*" (Heb. 1:3; C.R.).

Here He is no victim, but the Omnipotent One, effecting our purgation from sin, and having accomplished this He sits down at the Father's right hand.

Similarly He is seen in Heb. 10:12,14, not being offered in sacrifice, but *offering* one all-sufficient sacrifice by which His people are "perfected forever."

Thus again the Apostle depicts Him, not nailed to the cross by the law which we had broken, but as

44

Himself *nailing the law to His cross*, thus cancelling its claim and taking it out of the way for us, at the same time disarming Satan and his hosts and "leading them away in triumph" by it (See Col. 2:14,15; *C.R.*).

This is why Paul's "preaching of the cross" is called *"the gospel [good news] of the glory of Christ"* (II Cor. 4:4; *C.R.*). And this explains why Paul, unlike Peter at Pentecost, gloried, or boasted, in the cross (Gal. 6:14; *C.R.*).

We must not forget that those who first crucified Christ as their Victim were called upon to repent of their sin, and the only reason they were shown even this mercy was because the Lord Himself had prayed for them from the cross: *"Father forgive them, for they do not know what they are doing"* (Luke 23:34; *C.R.*).

And now, after the death of Christ has been revealed as the glorious victory by which He overcame sin and Satan and death and cancelled the claims of the law, shall priests bring Him down from heaven again and place Him on an altar as a victim, to slay Him in sacrifice for sin? Now that He has been exalted far above every name that is named as the Head over all (Eph. 1:20-22), shall *any* man have "jurisdiction" over Him?

In Hebrews 10 the Apostle Paul draws a striking contrast not only between the many Old Testament priests and our one great Priest, but also between the sacrifices constantly repeated by these priests and the all-sufficient, once-for-all sacrifice offered by our blessed Lord.

"And every priest indeed stands daily ministering, and often

45

offering the same sacrifices, which can never take away sins; but Jesus, having offered one sacrifice for sins, has taken His seat forever at the right hand of God . . . .for by one offering He has perfected forever those who are sanctified" (Heb. 10:11-14; C.R.).

What contrasts! Many priests; *one* Priest! Many sacrifices; *one* sacrifice! The many "can never take away sins"; the *one* takes them away completely and "perfects forever" those who are sanctified!

Indeed, it was the constant repetition of Old Testament sacrifices that in itself bore witness to their inability to take away the condemnation of sin, for the Apostle rightly argues that if it were otherwise: " . . .in that case would they not have ceased to be offered . . .?" (Heb. 10:2; *C.R.*).

Thus again the Apostle says of Christ ("such a high priest") that:

"He does not need to offer sacrifices daily (as the other priests did) first for His own sins, and then for the sins of the people; for this latter He did once for all in offering up Himself" (Heb. 7:26,27; C.R.).

The above passages and many more which we might produce from Roman Catholic versions of the Bible emphasize the all-sufficiency of the *one* sacrifice which our Lord offered for sin. To offer other sacrifices or to pretend to offer this one again and again can only insult the Omnipotent One who in one mighty stroke bore the penalty for sins that would have sunk a world to hell. Indeed the insult is the greater when these sacrifices are associated with the memorial of His accomplished redemption.

46

Not once in the Scriptures is the Lord's Supper called a sacrifice or associated with an altar or a priest. To turn it into a "sacrifice" is to rob it of the glory of its essential nature as a glad celebration of the *finished* and *all-sufficient* redemption wrought by Christ at Calvary.

Chapter V

The Lutheran View
of the Lord's Supper

LUTHER'S REPUDIATION
OF THE SACRIFICE OF THE MASS

Martin Luther repudiated many of Rome's inventions regarding the Lord's Supper, and it is like a refreshing breeze to read his strong Scriptural arguments for the all-sufficiency of Christ's finished work of redemption.

Denouncing "the Babylonian captivity of the Church" under Rome, especially with regard to the Lord's Supper, he contended that the "Sacrifice of the Mass," offered by the priests of Rome, falsely implied that man could do a work which God would accept as a satisfaction for sin. He declared that such "sacrifices" were "contrary to the Word of God," since "Christ's one sacrifice has made full atonement for *all sins*." Repudiating the teachings of Rome in this matter, he held that the Lord's Supper was rather the renewal of a pledge wherein God promises to us forgiveness of sins through Christ's death at Calvary and that this pledge can be accepted by faith and faith alone.

He repudiated, too, the Roman doctrine of *transubstantiation*, i.e., that upon its consecration by the priest "the substance of bread and wine ceases to be" and is "changed into Christ's body and blood, soul and divinity." This, he contended, was unscriptural, since "the Bible expressly declares that bread and wine are still present in the sacrament (I Cor. 10:16; 11:26-28)."

Luther further opposed as superstitious and idolatrous the teaching that the communicants at the Lord's Supper should *adore* the host and the chalice, and contended that salvation is to be found, not in partaking of the physical elements used, but by faith in the words of our Lord: *"given and shed for you for the remission of sins."* He also contended that *all*, not only the priest, should partake of the cup as well as of the bread, since our Lord said to His disciples: "Drink ye *all* of it" (Matt. 26:27).

We should thank God for opening Martin Luther's eyes to see the basic fallacies in Rome's "Sacrifice of the Mass" and for his boldness in holding this idolatrous practice up to the light of Scripture.

This is not to say, however, that Luther found his way completely out of the Roman woods, even with regard to this particular subject.

THE SACRAMENT OF THE ALTAR
AND CONSUBSTANTIATION

LUTHER'S ROMAN RAGS

While Martin Luther boldly denounced the so-called "Sacrifice of the Mass" with its doctrine of *transubstantiation* and the adoration of the host and chalice, he did not cast off all the rags of Rome where the Lord's Supper is concerned.

He himself called the Lord's Supper "the Sacrament of the Altar," and if there is an altar, why not a sacrifice, or if no sacrifice, why an altar?

THE REAL PRESENCE

Further, while repudiating Rome's doctrine of *transubstantiation*, he himself still taught the "real presence" of "the true body and blood" of Christ "in, with and under" the bread and wine. This is called *consubstantiation*, or the *union* of the two substances.

Luther's "Small Catechism" asks the question: "What is the Sacrament of the Altar?" and answers: "It is the true body and blood of our Lord Jesus Christ under the bread and wine, for us Christians to eat and drink, instituted by Christ Himself."

It has been said of the Catholic doctrine of *transubstantiation*, that after all the arguments advanced to make it sound reasonable, it is evident that Rome is actually contending for superstitious belief in magic.

We agree with this, but feel that Luther by no means entirely rid himself of this superstition in substituting *consubstantiation* for *transubstantiation*.

Remember that Luther contended—as Lutherans do today—for the *"real presence"* of Christ's *"true BODY and BLOOD"* "in, with and under" the bread and wine.

But no actual flesh and blood is, or can be, found in the elements Lutherans use at the Lord's Supper, and if chemically analyzed they would be found to be bread and wine alone. No trace of flesh or blood would be found. Are Lutherans, then, much less superstitious about this than Roman Catholics?

The reasons Lutherans give for believing in the real presence of Christ's body and blood in the bread and wine are as follows:

1. Like Rome, they argue that our Lord, as He instituted the supper, said: "This *is* My body" and "This *is* My blood" (*A Short Explanation of Dr. Martin Luther's Small Catechism*, Concordia Publ. House, P. 195).

To this we reply as we did in the case of the Roman Catholic argument, that the word "is" often means "represents" in the New Testament Scriptures, and *must* mean this here since our Lord was Himself present with them *in the flesh* when He gave them the bread and wine and said: "This is My body" and "This is My blood."

2. They point out that I Cor. 10:16 states that "the cup is the *communion* of the blood of Christ and that the bread is the *communion* of the body of Christ" (*Ibid.* Pp. 195,196).

But neither the wording here, nor the Greek from which it is taken, necessarily indicates that the body and blood of Christ are present in the bread and wine. The idea is simply that the saints, at the Lord's Supper, commune with each other concerning the breaking of Christ's body and the shedding of His blood for them.

3. We are reminded that I Cor. 11:27 teaches "that *unworthy communicants are guilty*, not of the bread and wine, but *of the body and blood of Christ*" (*Ibid*, P. 196).

To this we reply, *Of course!* Those partaking unworthily of a celebration of Christ's death on the cross would be guilty—not of despising the bread and wine, but of despising the body and blood of Christ which were broken and shed for their sins. This passage by no means proves that Christ's actual body and blood are present in the bread and wine.

4. We are warned that "no man has the right·to change the meaning of a divine institution and testament" (*Ibid*, P. 196).

We agree with this, but hold that both the Roman and Lutheran churches, rather than we, have changed the meaning of the divine institution.

The reader is urged here to look back at our arguments against *transubstantiation*, for many of them apply to *consubstantiation* as well.

PARTAKING OF CHRIST'S FLESH AND BLOOD

We remind our readers that *Luther's Small Catechism*, from which we have quoted, states that "the Sacrament of the Altar" is "the true body and blood of our Lord Jesus Christ . . .for us Christians to eat and drink . . . ."

Like the Roman Catholic Church, Luther and the Lutherans have based this doctrine on our Lord's words in John 6:51-56 about eating His flesh and drinking His blood to receive eternal life. Indeed, it appears that they would have had as little trouble as we do with His words: "This is My body" and "This is My blood," had it not been for the strong statements about eating Christ's flesh and drinking His blood, in John 6. We have already dealt with this passage at some length, but would point out here how Luther evidently did not—and *could not*—believe *without qualification*, what he wrote in his *Small Catechism* as quoted above.

DOUBLE TALK AGAIN

When theologians have presented arguments which do not make clear sense, they frequently lapse into double talk in trying to justify, or to qualify, what they have said.

Luther had come far enough out of Roman superstition to know that his statements about eating Christ's flesh and drinking His blood *had* to be qualified. Physical eating and drinking—even of Christ's flesh and blood—could not save a soul, nor would God have us entertain so repugnant and blasphemous a thought as that of actually eating and drinking the flesh and blood of His holy and beloved Son. Furthermore, how could millions, down through the ages, *all* eat and drink Christ's physical flesh and blood?

Clearly, Luther realized this, yet the traditional teaching regarding John 6 stuck with him and so, like the Roman theologians, he was forced to "explain" himself by double talk.

The declaration that in the Lord's Supper "the true body and blood" of Christ is *"in, with and under"* the bread and wine is already an example of this double talk, for how can it be *in* and *with* or *under* at the same time? The fact is that no trace of Christ's "true body and blood" can be found either in, with or under the bread and wine. But there is much more of this confused phraseology in Luther's doctrine of "the Sacrament of the Altar."

For example, after declaring that "the Sacrament of the Altar" is *"the true body and blood* of our Lord Jesus Christ . . .for us Christians *to eat and drink,"* (our

53

emphasis) his *Small Catechism* also contains the following questions and answers:

"What is the benefit of such eating and drinking?

"That is shown us by these words, 'Given and shed for you for the remission of sins'; namely, that in the Sacrament forgiveness of sins, life, and salvation are given us through these words. For where there is forgiveness of sins, there is also life and salvation."

Mark well that his *question* relates to "the benefit of such *eating and drinking*" and the answer is that "in the Sacrament forgiveness of sins, life, and salvation are given us ...." But he then confuses this by closing the sentence: "are given us *through these words.*"

Now it is true that the animal sacrifices of Old Testament times did not in themselves make the offerer acceptable to God. It was only as an expression of faith that they did so, and this might well be the same with the Lord's Supper, were it not that the Lord's Supper is clearly a remembrance of the *finished* work of Christ, and Luther himself was one of the foremost champions of the glorious all-sufficiency of Christ's accomplished redemption and of the fact that in the light of this, salvation is now specifically declared to be wholly by grace through faith, *apart from works.*

He was evidently convicted that physical eating and drinking, even in deepest sincerity, could not bring salvation, for in the next question and answer he presses this further:

"How can bodily eating and drinking do such great things?

"It is not the eating and drinking indeed that does them, but the *words* here written . . . which words, besides the bodily eating and drinking, are the chief thing in the Sacrament . . . ." (*Ibid*).

Thus he first says that forgiveness, life and salvation are the benefits of "such *eating and drinking.*" Then he says (in the same sentence) that "in the Sacrament" forgiveness, life and salvation are given us "through these words," (i.e., "Given and shed for you," etc.). Then he emphasizes this further by saying: "It is *not* the eating and drinking" that does these things, but confuses this again by declaring that *the words, "besides the bodily eating and drinking,* are the chief thing in the Sacrament."

Similarly, *A Short Explanation of Dr. Martin Luther's Small Catechism* has this to say about *how* we should partake of these elements which are supposed to contain both bread and wine and "the true body and blood" of Christ:

In the Supper, says this "explanation," the "bread and wine are received by the communicant *like any other food*, in a *natural manner*." But "Christ's body and blood are received by the communicant with *his mouth*, but in a *supernatural manner*" (P. 198, all emphasis theirs).

Here the physical and the spiritual, the natural and the supernatural are really confused! How can the mouth receive *physical* food (the "true *body* and *blood* of Christ") in a *supernatural* manner? Or, if it be argued that the body and blood of Christ are present only in a spiritual or supernatural way, how can the *mouth* receive them? This is called "sacramental eating and drinking," (*Ibid*, P. 198) but this writer would like to know just what "*sacramental* eating and drinking" is. Many a teaching which is contrary to both reason and the Word of God is advanced in vague phraseology—often successfully, because many sincere people think that a doctrine they cannot understand is probably either too far above them or too "deep" to grasp.

The sad thing about this unscriptural teaching is that it leads many simple and sincere people into superstition rather than faith. It leads them to suppose that going through a religious form will save, or at least help to save their souls, for this impression is certainly given, as for example in the question and answer: "For what purpose, then do we approach the Lord's table? . . .Chiefly to receive forgiveness of our sins . . ." (*Ibid*, P. 200). True, the answer goes on to list the strengthening of our faith, the obtaining of strength for a holier life and witnessing that we are of one faith with those who commune with us, but mark well that forgiveness of sins heads the list of the "chief" things we approach the table to obtain. Think of this in the light of the Pauline Scriptures as to salvation:

"Not by works of righteousness which we have done, but according to His mercy He saved us . . . ." (Tit. 3:5).

"For by one offering He hath perfected forever them that are sanctified" (Heb. 10:14).

Thank God, Luther truly believed in salvation by

grace, through faith, apart from works, religious or otherwise, but his views on the Lord's Supper were confused and inconsistent with this. It is often difficult to divest one's self of tradition and traditional interpretations, and this leads to such inconsistencies.

Chapter VI

Zwingli and Calvin
on
The Lord's Supper

ULRICH ZWINGLI

Zwingli left the Church of Rome even farther behind than did Luther with respect to the Lord's Supper.

He not only repudiated Rome's *Sacrifice of the Mass* and the doctrine of *transubstantiation*, but also Luther's *Sacrament of the Altar* and the doctrine of *consubstantiation*, rejecting altogether the idea of the *real presence* of Christ's flesh and blood at the Lord's Supper.

He held, as we do, that the word *is*, in "This is My body . . .My blood," means "signifies" or "represents," as it does in so many other places in Scripture.

In 1529 he and Luther met with Melanchthon and Oecolampadius at Marburg in an effort to resolve their dispute over this question. They were able to agree on fourteen articles of faith, but remained in disagreement on the question of the *real presence*.

JOHN CALVIN

John Calvin, it would seem, sought to effect a compromise between the position of Luther and Zwingli. At any rate, he took a position between the two and in doing so was, like Luther and the Church of Rome, forced to explain himself by double talk.

Calvin agreed with Zwingli that the bread and wine were only *signs* or *symbols* of our Lord's body and blood and that these were not actually present in the Lord's Supper. We quote a few passages from his *Institutes* and other writings on this subject

> "Thus Christ bestows upon the faithful receiver of the sacrament not, indeed, the substance, but the saving power of His body" (*Tracts and Treatises*, under *Short Treatise on the Lord's Supper*).

> "...it is not the very substance of the body, or the true and natural body of Christ that is there given, but all the benefits which Christ by His body has procured for us" (*Ibid*).

> "So, when bread is given to us as a symbol of the body of Christ....When we see wine presented as a symbol of His blood..." (*Institutes*, IV, XVII, 3).

BUT...

Calvin *also* taught that those who partake in faith of the supper *do* partake of Christ's *flesh* and *blood* in a mystical way. Not only did he call the bread and wine the "instruments whereby grace is imparted to the faithful receivers," but he insisted that in partaking of the bread and wine, the faithful actually partake of Christ's flesh and blood. We already find a hint of this idea in the phrase "the saving power of His *body*" (our italics) above, but his writings contain much stronger statements on this question:

> "The body, therefore, which was once offered for our salvation, we are commanded to

take and eat . . . .He presents us that sacred blood to drink" (*Institutes*, IV, XVII, 1).

But if the bread and wine are but *symbols* of Christ's body and blood, how can it be said that in partaking of them we partake of His *flesh* and *blood?* We can see how in the supper we may partake of Christ in a spiritual sense as the bread and the cup *represent* to us His broken body and shed blood and we remember that He was crucified *for us*, but this is not partaking of His *flesh and blood*. Says Calvin:

> "The signs are bread and wine, which represent to us the invisible nourishment which we receive from *the body and blood* of Christ" (*Institutes*, IV, XVII, 1, our emphasis).

STILL MORE DOUBLE TALK

But we protest that this is double talk. The nourishment we receive from partaking of physical food is something altogether different from the spiritual nourishment we receive from contemplating what Christ has done for us. Had Calvin used the word "spiritual" rather than "invisible" here, his inconsistency would immediately have appeared. The nourishment we derive from partaking of physical food may be "invisible," but it is *physical, not spiritual.*

Again: " . . .this mystical benediction is designed . . . to assure us that the *body* of the Lord was once offered as a sacrifice for us, *so that we may now feed upon it* . . ." (*Institutes*, IV, XVII, 1, our emphasis). This is as unreasonable as it is unscriptural, for our Lord's body came forth from the grave in resurrection glory and is now seated at the right hand of God in heaven.

60

While on the one hand repudiating the doctrine of the *real presence*, Calvin still declared:

> "In the mystery of the supper, under the symbols of the bread and wine, Christ is truly exhibited to us, *even His body and blood*, in which He has fulfilled all obedience to procure our justification" (*Institutes*, IV, XVII, 11, our emphasis).

What is this but Christ's *real presence* at the supper?

Again:

> "The bread is given us to figure the body of Jesus Christ, with command to eat it . . . .If God cannot deceive or lie, it follows that it accomplishes all which it signifies. We must then truly receive in the supper *the body and blood of Jesus Christ* . . . .If He gave us only bread and wine, leaving *the spiritual reality* behind, would it not be under false colors that this ordinance had been instituted?" (*Tracts and Treatises*, under "Short Treatise on the Lord's Supper," our emphasis).

Mark well how he here confuses the physical and the spiritual. In the supper, he argues, we must truly receive Christ's *body and blood*, otherwise *the spiritual reality* would be left behind!

Thus such phrases as *"the mystery of the sacred supper"* come to mean in fact, not merely that we must accept a doctrine that is *beyond* human understanding, but one that is contrary to reason, that is illogical and inconsistent with itself.

True, Calvin was careful to teach that only the faithful participant in the Lord's Supper actually partakes of Christ's flesh and blood, since "the life-giving virtue of Christ's glorified body is . . .diffused by the Holy Spirit" to believers alone (See his notes on I Cor. 11:24). But this in no wise alters the fact that in the Calvinistic observance of the Lord's Supper there is still a great element of mysticism and superstition.

Chapter VII

The "Plymouth Brethren" and the Lord's Supper

We have yet to consider the views of the so-called "Plymouth Brethren" [1] with regard to the Lord's Supper, before dealing with the views of those who do not believe in observing it.

Correctly the "Brethren" consider the Lord's Supper a *commemoration* of our Lord's death and deny the doctrines of transubstantiation and consubstantiation. There are some aspects of their celebration of the Supper, however, for which we can find no solid Scriptural support.

THE BREAKING OF BREAD

Those who have had close association with the "Brethren," as this writer has, [2] know that whereas other believers generally refer to the celebration in question as "the Lord's supper," or "the Lord's table," or "communion," the "Brethren" usually refer to it as "the breaking of bread." This, we feel, is because they have read the Lord's Supper *into* several passages where it is not necessarily referred to.

---

1. Some of these prefer to be called simply "brethren," with a small "b," but this designation would fail to distinguish them from those brethren in and out of the various denominations who differ with them as to the Lord's Supper and other doctrines.

2. We shall always thank our Heavenly Father for the fellowship we have enjoyed with these dear saints and for the blessings received through their ministry of the Word.

The "breaking of bread" in Acts 2:42 is generally supposed to refer to the Lord's Supper, but there is no clear evidence that this is so. Food and fellowship are often found together in Scripture (See Luke 15:2, *et al*) thus the "fellowship" and "breaking of bread" in this passage may simply refer to their dining together, since they had so much in common at that time. Indeed, this is the more probable in view of the following verses, which relate how they "were together, and had all things common," and that "continuing in the temple and *breaking bread from house to house* [they] did *eat their meat* [*food*] with gladness and singleness of heart" (Vers. 44-46).

Neither does Acts 20:7 necessarily refer to the Lord's Supper. The brethren at Troas may well have chosen this time to enjoy each other's fellowship around a common table since this may have been the only time when working conditions made this possible. And certainly Acts 27:35 was not a celebration of the Lord's Supper.

The "breaking of bread" was a term popularly used to designate a common meal. Our Lord was made known to the two Emmaus disciples in the "breaking of bread," but surely this was not a celebration of the Lord's Supper. Indeed, our Lord was Host in the breaking of bread to about 5,000 guests at one time and about 4,000 at another (Mark 6:41; 8:6) and these events took place considerably before He even instituted the Supper.

In this connection it should also be observed that it was as natural at that time to speak of dining as the "breaking of *bread*," as it is now to speak of it as "eating," simply because on such occasions we generally consume more food than drink.

This is not so with regard to the Lord's Supper. Here *two* elements share *equal* importance, the bread symbolizing our Lord's body and the wine His blood. We do not feel, therefore, that our "Brethren" are on solid Scriptural ground in referring to the Lord's Supper as the "breaking of bread."

MUST THE LORD'S SUPPER BE OBSERVED EVERY WEEK?

Their interpretation of Acts 20:7 has led the "Brethren" to assume that believers are to observe the Lord's Supper on the first day of each week. This has almost taken on the form of a law with them. We have known some of them, when alone and away from a "Brethren" assembly on a Sunday morning, to obtain bread and wine and hold "communion" all by themselves. This took place in the guest room of our home on several occasions.

We feel that this insistence on a *weekly* observance of the Lord's Supper is wrong on two counts.

First, even *if* the "breaking of bread" in Acts 20:7 referred to the celebration of the Lord's Supper, it would not follow from this that *other* believers were obliged to celebrate the Supper exactly when and as often as the believers at Troas did. Our Lord, when He instituted the Supper for His disciples, made no stipulation as to time or frequency of observance, and certainly Paul, who "delivered" the celebration to us, left the matter entirely open to grace, using the words

65

"as oft," simply assuming that believers would wish to take part in this celebration from time to time. At any rate, our "Brethren" are surely not on solid Scriptural ground in advancing Acts 20:7 as proof that *the Lord's Supper* should be "observed" weekly on the first day of the week. Neither this passage nor any other says anything of the kind.

What is perhaps more serious, however, is that the "Brethren" view has, as we say, taken on almost the force of a law, and has become so binding as to create such circumstances as we have described above. To most of them the Lord's Supper *must* be "observed" on the first day of *every* week.

This is legalism, one result of which is that to many of us the "observance" of the Lord's Supper at "Brethren" assemblies has seemed oversolemn and lacking in the worshipful joy that should characterize a celebration of what our glorious Lord accomplished for us at Calvary.

CLOSED COMMUNION

Finally, we feel that those "Brethren" who hold to what is known as "closed communion" lack Scriptural support for their practice. A brother in Christ, who lives consistently and labors earnestly for his Lord, must remain in the "outer circle" and is refused a place at the Lord's table, simply because he does not belong to "the brethren" or to their particular brand of "brethren."

Perhaps it was this sort of thing that John Darby had in mind when, reportedly, he said: "When the

66

brethren shall have become a sec: they will be of all sects most sectarian."

True, when all know that a professing Christian is a disgrace to Christ because of his wayward life, discipline must be taken, and for this the Scriptures make provisions.   But apart from this, who are *we* to judge which believers may have a place at the *Lord's* table and which may not?   The Apostle Paul declares by the Spirit: *"Let a man examine HIMSELF, and so let him eat of that bread and drink of that cup"* (I Cor. 11:28). Surely the truly spiritual saint, remembering Calvary, will be slow to judge another and quick to judge himself where worthiness to partake of the Lord's Supper is concerned.

We thank God that there appears to be a trend toward a more Scriptural view of the Lord's Supper among many of the "Brethren."   We pray it may continue, for we have always regarded them as saints who truly love the Word.

Chapter VIII

The Quakers, The Salvation Army And the Lord's Supper

The *Salvation Army* and the *Quakers* [1] or *Society of Friends* hold that our Lord did not intend that the Lord's Supper should be observed physically by the Church. They do not, however, conclude that this celebration is unscriptural *per se*.

THE QUAKERS

Howard Brinton, in his book *Friends for 300 Years*, has stated:

> "There is nothing in *Quaker* theory which would categorically exclude such rites as baptism and communion, provided these were, when experienced, genuine outward expressions of real and holy inward states."

It is rather from a fear that the observance of an outward form may detract from a true spiritual experience that the *Quakers* have eliminated both water baptism and the Lord's Supper from their practice.

It was as George Fox, founder of the *Society of Friends*, observed 17th century Protestantism and saw how the use of the "sacraments" had become an end in itself, that he and the *Friends* eliminated both baptism and the Lord's Supper from their church program. In

---

1. This name is not used in any derogatory sense. The *Friends* call themselves *Quakers* in many of their writings.

the words of Robert E. Cope, they were "determined that nothing should be resorted to which would come between the soul of man and his Maker" (*What About the Sacraments?*, P. 2) Cope further points out that it is not the intention of the *Quakers* to underestimate in any way the spiritual reality for which these "sacraments" stood (*Ibid*, P. 5).

THE SALVATION ARMY

Since 1960 the *Salvation Army* has published an official defense of its position on *"The Sacraments,"* inscribed only with the words: "Issued by authority of *The General*." Like the *Friends*, the *Salvation Army* does not condemn the celebration of the Lord's Supper *per se*, for this book states:

"We never declaim against the sacraments," said William Booth [2] to Henry Lunn, an Army friend in the early days. "We are anxious not to destroy the confidence of Christian people in institutions which are helpful to them" (P. 19).

The *Army's* book on *"The Sacraments"* is exceedingly well written and, like *Quaker* literature on the subject, contains some propositions and arguments which are not only valid, but blessedly true.

There is, for example, the quotation from Catherine Booth:

"What an inveterate tendency there is in the human heart to trust in outward forms, instead of seeking the inward grace. And where this is the case, what a hindrance, rather than help have these forms proved...."

---

2. Founder of the *Salvation Army.*

"Nothing is more evident to all who have any acquaintance with the history of Christianity, than that the undue value set upon these ceremonies has been one of the greatest hindrances to the extension of Christianity..." (Pp. 8,9).

There is also the following quotation from the writings of the well-known Baptist, Professor H. H. Rowley. Here Professor Rowley concedes:

"The symbol is of less importance than that which it symbolizes. It is of importance that Baptists, no less than others, should remember this. What matters most is not that a man has been voluntarily immersed any more than that he has been baptized in infancy, but that he has truly died with Christ and been raised again to newness of life in Him . . . The symbol is worthless without that which it symbolizes" (P. 9).

All this, says *"The Sacraments,"* "brings us to the fundamental truth" that Christianity is "essentially spiritual" and "not essentially ritualistic," and that "it can and does exist—and very often thrives—without any ritual expression" (P. 10).

"God is wherever there is spiritual need, wherever human hearts cry out to Him" (P. 16).

Thus *"The Sacraments"* claims, "with the early Quakers":

"We do not make use of the outward rites of Baptism and the Lord's Supper, but we do believe in the experiences they symbolize.

Our testimony is to the actuality of this experience without the external rite" (P. 18).

"The heart-searching question to which Salvationists have always had to submit their lives is *not*: Ought I regularly to participate in the Lord's Supper as a religious ceremony? It has always been and is: Is there a real communion between myself and my Lord? Do I possess His Spirit and do His will? Those who survive the scrutiny of the latter can dispense with the former question, and can do so without feeling that they are in any way disregarding any command of Christ" (P. 52).

WHERE WE AGREE AND DISAGREE

Apart from questions as to the ritual and the real, we agree that water baptism should be eliminated from our practice as members of the Body of Christ, since it belonged to another dispensation and was required for "the remission of sins" (Mark 1:4; 16:16; Acts 2:38; 22:16).

We even agree that the Lord's Supper *as practiced* by most in the 17th century and through the centuries until this day, is *utterly unscriptural* and tends to foster religious superstition rather than faith and spirituality.

We do not agree, however, that therefore the communion of the Lord's Supper should be eliminated, for this celebration, unlike the ordinance of water baptism, was delivered to believers of the present dispensation, and members of the "one Body" (I Cor. 12:13) to celebrate *"till He come"* (I Cor. 11 23-26).

71

It is *our* fault, not God's, if we make of the Lord's Supper a solemn sacrament which is meant to accomplish something for us, rather than the grateful celebration of our Lord's death in our behalf which it was meant to be. Hence it is as dishonoring to God to eliminate this celebration from our practice as it is to pervert it.

The question whether we *need* the outward form to hold communion with our Lord is beside the point, since it is God's expressed will that we take part in the Lord's Supper as a celebration of His finished work.

DID OUR LORD INSTITUTE THE COMMUNION SUPPER?

Since the founding of the *Salvation Army*, nearly 100 years ago, most of its members have somehow been convinced that our Lord never instituted the communion service as something to be observed again and again. An argument from Scripture which has been used comparatively recently to prove this, however, should be considered here. Says *"The Sacraments"*:

"Only Luke records the words: 'This do in remembrance of Me.' . . .Some time ago (in the last century) New Testament scholars discovered that in several early manuscripts of the New Testament—what is known as the "Western Text," and six of the most ancient Latin versions—Luke's account is shorter than the later manuscripts from which all our translations come. The second part of Verse 19 (from "which is given for you") and the whole of Verse 20 are missing (Pp. 47,48).

"It is known that manuscripts are sometimes added to, but nothing of such importance as this would have been omitted without good reason" (P. 48).

We have two answers to this argument. First, we challenge the statement that while "manuscripts are sometimes added to...nothing of such importance as this would have been omitted without good reason." On the contrary, it would be much more natural for a copyist to overlook a passage than to take it upon himself to add to the Holy Scriptures. While the authenticity of Luke 22:19*b* and 20 might be debated by some, the above consideration would argue *for* its authenticity.

Our second answer revolves around the explanation of *"The Sacraments"* for the presence of the debated words in the *Authorized* Version of Luke 22. We quote:

"From whence did these verses find their way into the later copies of Luke's Gospel? We have not far to look, for I Cor. 11:23-26 provides the answer" (P. 49).

Now in this passage Paul, by inspiration, clearly states that our Lord *did* say *"this do in remembrance of Me."* Why, then, try to prove from Luke 22 that He did *not* institute the Lord's Supper as a remembrance, simply on the grounds that these words *may* not be in the original *in that passage?*

After quoting I Cor. 11:23-26 in full, the author of *"The Sacraments"* actually by-passes the words *"this do in remembrance of Me,"* to point out that with regard to the cup, our Lord said: "This do ye, *as oft as ye drink it*, in remembrance of Me." "Here," says the author, "is no command necessarily relating to a formal ceremonial" (P. 50).

The words "as oft as ye drink it" would, to this writer at least, indicate two things: 1.) that this "remembrance" *was* to be observed repeatedly, and 2.) that, unlike the rituals of the Old Testament, it was *not* an *ordinance*, with specific rules as to just how and when to observe it.

As to our second answer above, the words "For as often as ye eat this bread and drink this cup" would appear to indicate that rather than commanding the observance of the Lord's Supper as an ordinance to be kept at certain specific times, the apostle of grace assumes that believers will wish, from time to time, to take part in this glad celebration of the glorious finished work of our Lord.

Finally, while it is true that believers may not need outward forms to hold communion with their Lord, the Lord's Supper was not "delivered" to us by our Apostle Paul for our sakes alone. It was to be a *public* celebration, held, not in homes, but at public gatherings to "*show* the Lord's death, till He come."

Chapter IX

The Lord's Supper
and Extreme Dispensationalism

In the early days of the so-called "Grace Movement," many sincere believers were thrilled as they learned to study the Bible dispensationally. As, by God's grace, they began to see the distinctions between Paul's message and that previously proclaimed by Peter and the eleven, between the kingdom of heaven and the Body of Christ, the so-called "great commission" and our greater commission, the Rapture of the Body and the revelation of Christ, etc., they began to *understand* the Bible, and hence *enjoy* it, as never before. Seeming discrepancies began to disappear and the truths of Scripture began to fall into their proper places and assume their proper proportions.

But then, as the pendulum naturally swings from one extreme position to the other some dispensationalists went to the opposite extreme from the errors of traditionalism from which they had been delivered and arrived at the most strained and radical interpretations of Scripture. Puzzled over some aspects of Paul's early ministry, they began finding distinctions which did not actually exist. Seeking to account for some of Paul's early teachings and actions, some concluded that he evidently did not receive the revelation of the mystery until his imprisonment at Rome—though he himself claimed to be in bonds for having proclaimed the mystery! This error forced them to conclude further that *two* special ministries were committed to him, that there must be *two* Bodies of Christ, etc.

The significance of Paul's early epistles to us was, of course, directly involved. The intercessory work of Christ, the throne of grace, the Rapture of I Thes. 4 and I Cor. 15 and the celebration of the Lord's Supper—all these, they said, belonged to Paul's "kingdom ministry," not his ministry to us as members of the joint Body. Of course they could not apply to us because they were found in his *early* epistles!

This all sounded interesting but it could not stand the Berean test. It raised more questions than it answered. Everywhere there were loose ends, for if there is one factor of Scripture these brethren did *not* see in their studies it is the grand sweep, the progress, the development in God's majestic program of the ages.

In the providence of God, however, this issue was met head on and discussed at length and thoroughly, both publicly and privately. Those who thus divided Paul's special ministry into two were so fully and conclusively answered that the grace movement once more began to make real progress, the majority of "grace" believers standing firmly for the distinctive character of the great Pauline revelation, *gradually* committed to him by the glorified Son of God in heaven.

Due, however, to the tendency among men—even men of God—to stand by their teachings and writings, no matter how conclusively disproven, and due also to the natural tendency of those coming out of traditionalism to swing to the other extreme, some of these radical and unscriptural teachings are still, or again, finding acceptance among some sincere Bible students.

Since both doctrine and practice are affected by these teachings, especially where the Lord's Supper is concerned, we have felt that it might prove helpful to many if we presented the following discussion of the Lord's Supper and extreme dispensationalism.

THE LORD'S SUPPER
AND OUR HEAVENLY POSITION

We believe firmly that the celebration of the Lord's Supper was included in the great revelation committed by the glorified Lord to Paul and is therefore an integral part of the "one faith" to which he refers in Eph. 4:5, that body of doctrine to which all believers in this present dispensation of grace should subscribe.

Nevertheless we sympathize with many who sincerely love the Lord Jesus Christ, yet do not join with us in this blessed communion service. Many of these have come out of Roman Catholicism and naturally tend to associate the Lord's Supper with the Mass and all its superstition. Others have come from other denominations in which the observance of the Lord's Supper is considered necessary to the remission of sins and they feel that in the light of grace it would be a step backward to "observe" the Lord's Supper. Still others, who have come to rejoice in the riches of God's grace, can associate the Lord's Supper only with the dull, somber observances which they were called upon to endure in their former places of "worship," where the Supper was indeed held to be a memorial but "observed" as if it were a meritorious sacrament.

77

It is to such that we address this part of this book.

THE LORD'S SUPPER
A PHYSICAL CEREMONY

One basic argument generally advanced by these brethren runs somewhat as follows: The physical types of the Old Testament spoke of *spiritual* realities. Believers now *have* these realities in Christ. They are "blessed with all *spiritual* blessings *in the heavenlies* in Christ." Why, then, observe this one physical ceremony?

Now, it is indeed true that believers are "blessed with all spiritual blessings in the heavenlies," but this does not mean that somehow we have already been transformed into the spiritual beings we some day shall be. For the present we must occupy our heavenly position and appropriate our spiritual blessings *by faith* because perforce we still have much, very much, to do with the physical. In the very epistles of Paul, which tell us about our baptism into Christ and our position and blessings in Him, we learn about the significance of physical things, including our physical bodies, in our present Christian service and conduct.

We have already stated that we quite agree with the following observation by Catherine Booth:

"What an inveterate tendency there is in the human heart to trust in outward forms, instead of seeking the inward grace. And where this is the case, what a hindrance, rather than help have these forms proved . . . .

"Nothing is more evident to all who have any acquaintance with the history of Chris-

tianity, than that the undue value set upon
these ceremonies has been one of the greatest
hindrances to the extension of Christianity . . ." (*The Sacraments*, Pp. 8,9).

But could not all this have been said about the Old
Testament ceremonies as well? In fact, several of the
Old Testament prophets expressed the same senti-
ments with great emphasis as, for example, Isaiah,
when he called Judah's spiritual leaders the "rulers of
Sodom" and her people the "people of Gomorrah,"
telling them that God abhorred "the multitude of their
sacrifices," their solemn "treading of His courts" and
their "vain oblations"; warning them that the hypoc-
risy of their "appointed feasts" and "solemn meetings"
was a sin that He could not endure and would cause
Him to close His eyes and His ears when they "spread
forth their hands" to pray (See Isa. 1:10-15).

It does not follow from this, however, that God's
people of that day were relieved of bringing sacrifices
and oblations or of observing their appointed feasts.
The difficulty was that they had come to *trust* in these
things while ignoring spiritual values. Judah's abuse
or misunderstanding of her God-appointed ceremonies
did not constitute a license to stop practicing them.

In fact, we today are not to forbear observing the
Old Testament ordinances merely because they were
misunderstood or failed to produce results, but *because
they have been fulfilled in Christ.* [1]

If we today observed any ceremony which was once
required for acceptance with God we would be doing

---

1. This includes water baptism. See the author's book *Things That Differ.*

79

wrong, *not* because we were taking part in a physical ceremony but because participation in *such* a ceremony would cast reflections upon the *finished* work of Christ. This is where water baptism and the Lord's Supper, so often linked together, differ so widely in character, for water baptism was required for the remission of sins while the Lord's Supper is a glad "remembrance" of our Lord's finished work for the remission of sins and His fulfilling of the Old Testament ordinances.

It has always been difficult for us to follow the logic of those who hold that since our position and blessings are in the heavenlies we should not partake of the Lord's Supper because of the physical elements involved.

This is the same "logic" by which some sincere believers teach that it is wrong for Christians to vote in civil elections since "our citizenship is in heaven."

Paul's epistles warn against observing physical ordinances,[2] to be sure, but they do not teach, indeed, they refute the error that physical things are incompatible with spiritual blessings.

PHYSICAL PRIVILEGES AND SPIRITUAL BLESSINGS

There are many physical privileges which when rightly performed are translated into spiritual blessings. We may bow our physical knees unto the Father (Eph. 3:14) and approach Him in prayer. We may study physical Bibles (II Tim. 2:15) and come to under-

---

2. Things ordained, i.e., for acceptance with God.

stand and enjoy God's Word, which is "settled for ever in Heaven." We may "prove the sincerity of our love" by sacrificing of our physical means to further the cause of Christ (II Cor. 8:7,8). Indeed, we may—and should—offer even these physical *bodies* as "living sacrifices, holy, acceptable unto God" (Rom. 12:1). We may assemble physically at appointed times with other saints (Heb. 10:25) and enjoy spiritual fellowship as members of the Body of Christ. We may use physical hymn books as we join in singing "psalms and hymns and spiritual songs . . .making melody in our hearts to the Lord" (Eph. 5:19). And we may gather around the Lord's table, with its physical elements (I Cor. 11: 23-26) and "remember," and so come to appreciate more fully, what our blessed Lord did for us at Calvary.

To those who decline to participate in the celebration of the Lord's Supper we say sincerely that we are as much opposed to the *popular* "observance" of this so-called "sacrament" as they are, but we must be careful not to allow the failures of men to cause us to ignore clear instructions "delivered" to us by the Apostle Paul as he "received" them from the glorified Lord:

"For I have received of the Lord that which also I delivered unto you, That the Lord Jesus, the same night in which He was betrayed . . .said . . . .

" . . . .This do in remembrance of Me . . . .

"For as often as ye eat this bread, and drink this cup, ye do show the Lord's death till He come" (I Cor. 11:23-26).

81

Chapter X

Is the Lord's Supper
A Perpetuation of the Passover Feast?

We have before us a copy of *The Lord's Supper, A Prophetic Memorial*, published in 1960. While we sincerely respected the author's Christian character and love for the Word we have since, however, gotten out of touch with him, so forbear to name him.

This writer seeks to prove, as many extreme dispensationalists have done, that the Lord's Supper is not to be observed during the present dispensation of grace, but we believe it can be demonstrated that he has a way of going into a Scriptural subject *at length, but not carefully.* He gathers many details to put his argument across, but fails to think these details through.

Rejecting the view that the first Lord's Supper *followed* the Passover feast, he argues from the assumption that "...the Scriptures seem to teach that the Lord's Supper and the Jewish Passover are essentially one and the same..." (P. 6).

Now a "seem" here is wholly unsatisfactory, for this is the very core of the matter. Our brother ought to be able to give some definite Scriptural proof of this before he comes to such a conclusion, and certainly before he uses it in an argument against the present-day observance of the Lord's Supper.

THE LORD'S SUPPER NEVER
CALLED THE PASSOVER

The *fact* is that the Scriptures which relate to the Lord's Supper *never* call it the Passover, nor are we told *anywhere* in Scripture that the Lord's Supper is the same as the Passover. Nor again are we *anywhere* informed that the disciples were instructed to continue to celebrate the Passover as a memorial of Christ's death.

On the contrary, both in the "Gospels" and in Paul's account in I Cor. 11 the impression is clearly given that the Lord instituted a *new* ceremony as a memorial of His sacrificial death. Not a hint is given that the Passover was merely to be perpetuated.

For one thing, the Passover consisted of *roast lamb* and *unleavened* bread, eaten with *bitter herbs, not wine* (Ex. 12:8). This is not to deny, of course, that they may have drunk wine *in connection with* the Passover, but the Passover itself consisted of roast lamb, unleavened bread and bitter herbs, *not* bread and wine. For another thing, Luke 22:20 clearly states that our Lord took the communion cup *"after supper,"* and this was clearly also true of the communion bread, with which it is connected by the word *"likewise"* and by the fact that in I Cor. 11:23-25 the bread and the cup, as the two elements of the Lord's Supper, are also connected by the words: *"after the same manner."*

THE LAST PASSOVER

Next our brother *assumes* that "the Passover lamb was not present" at our Lord's last Passover "because the true lamb was with the disciples ..." (P. 6). But this assumption is wholly gratuitous and unwarranted. Our Lord, shortly before the feast day, had sent word to a friend, saying: "The Master saith, My time is at hand; I will keep the Passover at thy house with My disciples," and reading on, we learn that "the disciples did as Jesus had appointed them, and they made ready the Passover" (Matt. 26:18,19). Neither in this, nor in *any* passage is there *any* indication that our Lord instructed His disciples to omit the lamb, the most significant course of the meal. Indeed, the clear implication is that the lamb was included, for we read simply that "they made ready the Passover," *and this included roast lamb*. Had He meant to omit it He surely would have said so, for to His disciples—what would Passover be without the lamb? Yet, without a shred of Scriptural proof, our brother dogmatically states that the Passover lamb was not present at this last Passover.

His declaration that the Passover lamb was omitted "because the true lamb was with the disciples" is then straightway rendered invalid by his further statement: "and they partook of Him in a figure through the bread and the cup"! (P. 6). Pray tell, if they did not need the figure of the lamb, why the figures of the bread and wine? Did not these also speak of partaking of the results of His death; of feasting on His finished work?

FALSE PREMISE—FALSE CONCLUSIONS

On the mere—and untenable—assumption that the Lord's Supper was the Passover, perpetuated in a different manner, our brother bases further arguments:

84

1. That it (the Lord's Supper) was a Jewish ordinance (P. 6).

2. That it was to be observed once a year (P. 6).

3. That it was to be observed until our Lord's coming "in power and glory" to earth (Pp. 1,6).

4. That in view of Israel's rejection of the kingdom "the dispensation which included the Lord's Supper ended at Acts 28:25-28" (P. 4).

5. That we therefore should not practice it today (P. 6).

But his conclusions are as false as his premise.

THE CORINTHIANS NOT ISRAELITES

When Paul wrote to the Corinthian believers about the Lord's Supper, he wrote to them as a congregation of *Gentiles* in the flesh, *not* Israelites. Any converted Jews among them were clearly in the minority, for *immediately after* writing them about the Lord's Supper, the Apostle goes on to say:

"Ye know that ye were Gentiles, carried away unto these dumb idols . . ." (I Cor. 12:2).

And as to their looking for the Lord's coming in power to earth to reign, let the reader ask himself: Were these Gentile believers "marching to Zion" or were they on their way to heaven? As early as the first epistle to the Thessalonians Paul had already written about believers being *"caught up . . .to meet the Lord in the air"* to be forever "with the Lord" (I Thes. 4:17).

85

As to the termination of the Lord's Supper at Acts 28, consider this: Water baptism was *not* included in Paul's special ministry and he clearly indicates that the practice was to be terminated (I Cor. 1:17,18; Eph. 4:5; Heb. 9:10; *et al*). The Lord's Supper, however, *was* part of his special revelation ministry (I Cor. 11:23) and there is therefore the greater reason to believe that if its practice was to be terminated he would have informed us so. But he did not. On the contrary, he says that by this celebration *"ye do show the Lord's death TILL HE COME"* (I Cor. 11:26).

Seeking to make a Jewish and legal thing out of the Lord's Supper, our brother goes to great lengths to prove that unleavened bread and fermented wine must be used, otherwise the observance becomes "a repulsive perversion of the truth of God" (P. 3). Here is a striking example of his failure to think things through in the light of the Scriptures. The bread, he says, *"could not* contain leaven" (his italics) because in its nature it could not then typify our sinless Lord. This, he says, "is not a trivial matter" (P. 3). But on Page 6, where he argues for *fermented* wine, he seems to have completely forgotten his argument about leaven, for leaven, or yeast, is that which ferments! The very first definition for leaven in our Webster's Dictionary is: *"A substance that produces fermentation."*

It is entirely possible, perhaps even probable, that both unleavened bread and fermented wine were used at the Lord's table, but this was possible because these two elements were symbols only of the facts that His body was to be broken and His blood shed for us.

THE COMMUNION SERVICE,
BORING OR BLESSED?

We sympathize with many, perhaps including our brother, who have come from backgrounds in which the Lord's Supper is observed with a religious solemnity that amounts almost to gloom and with a legalism almost as stern as that which governed the observance of Old Testament rites. These often find it exceedingly difficult to understand how a physical ceremony (not ordinance) is compatible with the dispensation of the grace of God and our position in the heavenlies, and so they begin to seek answers to what the Scriptures so clearly say. But our brother's basic argument for the discontinuance of this celebration is a particularly serious departure from truth since, in starting a new Pauline dispensation at Acts 28, he and those who argue as he does divide the Epistles of Paul in two and neutralize the distinctive character of his ministry and gospel—both of which are spoken of in the singular in the Scriptures. This is as serious a mistake as that of those who hold that the "one Body" began at Acts 2 and confuse Paul's ministry with that of the twelve.

Those who have regarded the Lord's Supper in the light of the Pauline revelation, however, have again and again been drawn closer to Him by it. This solemn and precious memorial of the cross has made them more deeply conscious and more heartily thankful that to lift us from earth to "heavenly places in Christ" He had to leave heaven and live and die on this sin-cursed earth; that to bless us with "all spiritual blessings" He had to take upon Himself a physical

87

body, to be beaten and scourged and spit upon and crucified.

By these physical elements God would impress upon our hearts the great truth that:

"You that were sometime alienated and enemies in your mind by wicked works, yet now hath He reconciled *in the body of His flesh, through death*, to present you holy and unblamable and unreprovable in His sight" (Col. 1:21,22).

Yet nowhere does the Apostle make this celebration a legal ordinance. He rather assumes we will want to take part in it, saying:

"For as often as ye eat this bread, and drink this cup, ye do show the Lord's death till He come" (I Cor. 11:26).

May the Lord in His grace keep us always true to the Scriptures rightly divided. May He keep us balanced and give us the Spiritual power that comes with an understanding of the *sense* of Scripture, in its details as well as in its great basic teachings.

Chapter XI

The Lord's Supper
and The New Covenant

"Our sufficiency is of God; who a so hath made us able ministers of the new testament [covenant]."

—II Cor. 3:5,6

Some have supposed that since the Lord's Supper is related to the new covenant (I Cor. 11:25) it can have no place in the program of the Body of Christ.

But this is a mistake since, not only is it Paul who "delivered" the Lord's Supper to us Gentiles as a memorial of Christ's finished work, but it is Paul, *not Peter*, who calls himself an "able minister of the new covenant." This, simply because the mystery, or secret, had to be revealed before the prophecies could be fulfilled, and the secret of the new covenant, the basis for the fulfillment of *all* prophecy, was first revealed to Paul, not to Peter.

A TWOFOLD DANGER

Much harm and loss has come to the Church because God's "workmen" have failed to note the distinctions and divisions in the Word of truth. But serious harm can also result from a failure to recognize the *unity* of God's great plan for the ages; from a failure to observe *connections* as well as distinctions.

For example, there are some who, reading such a passage as the above, immediately conclude that it has nothing whatever to do with the Body of Christ. The

89

new covenant, they argue, was made with Israel; what relation can it have to the Body?

From this they further conclude that Paul, when he wrote these early epistles, could not yet have come into his special Gentile ministry; that at that time he had a Jewish-kingdom ministry, working under the "great commission" and preaching "the gospel of the circumcision."

And this when the Apostle himself, in these same *early* epistles, makes it clear that the gospel of the circumcision was *not* committed to him, but to Peter (Gal. 2:2,7-9); that *he* writes to *Gentiles* (Rom. 11:13; I Cor. 12:2; I Thes. 1:9); that these Gentiles were members of "the Body of Christ" (I Cor. 12:27) with a hope in *heaven* (I Thes. 1:10; 4:16-18)!

Thus our adversary again attacks the great Pauline message, seeking to keep us from *rightly* dividing the Word of truth and, if possible, robbing us of half our private mail.

THE NEW COVENANT AND US

But let us face the question. If the new covenant was indeed made with Israel, what relation can it have to members of the Body of Christ? Let us see:

First, is it true that the new covenant was made *exclusively* with the Hebrew nation? Yes, for Jer. 31:31 states:

"Behold, the days come, saith the Lord, that *I will make a new covenant with the house of Israel, and with the house of Judah.*"

But what was the nature of the new covenant? Let us see:

90

" . . .I will make a new covenant with the house of Israel, and with the house of Judah:

"Not according to the covenant that   made with their fathers in the day that I took them by the hand to bring them out of the land of Egypt; which My covenant they brake, although I was an husband unto them, saith the Lord.

"But this shall be the covenant that I will make with the house of Israel: After those days, saith the Lord, *I will put My law in their inward parts, and write it in their hearts; and will be their God, and they shall be My people.*

"*And they shall teach no more every man his neighbor, and every man his brother, saying, Know the Lord; for they shall all know Me, from the least of them unto the greatest of them, saith the Lord; for I will forgive their iniquity, and I will remember their sin no more*" (Jer. 31:31-34).

It should be carefully observed that this "new covenant" was *all* "spirit," not "letter," as the Apostle points out in II Cor. 3:6. In it there are no legal stipulations, nor any mention of a land, a kingdom or a throne, but rather of the forgiveness of sins, of knowing the Lord and of an imparted desire to do His will. [1] What Israel had failed to do under "the letter," she would be—and *will* be—impelled and enabled to do by *the Spirit.*

When and where was the new covenant made?

At Calvary, for in Mark 14:24 it is written:

"And He said unto them, *This is My blood of the new testament* [*covenant*], *which is shed for many.*"

---

1. It is noteworthy that Paul is never called a minister of the Abrahamic, Mosaic or Davidic covenants, but only of the new covenant.

The *making* of the new covenant, however, should not be confused with its *fulfillment*, for it will not be fulfilled until they *all* know the Lord, "from the least of them to the greatest of them."

Do members of the Body of Christ receive any of the blessings outlined in the new covenant?

Yes, *all* of them.

Has He not written His law upon *our* hearts? Is it not *our* desire to obey Him? Do *we* not "know the Lord," from the least of us to the greatest of us? Is He not *our* God? Are *we* not His people? Has He not forgiven *our* iniquities? Does He remember *our* sins against us?

Do we receive these blessings because they were in any way *promised* to us?

No; what was *promised* to Israel, we receive by *grace*. We receive these blessings because the blood of the new covenant was *also* shed for the sins of the world, *"that He might reconcile both [Jews and Gentiles] unto God in one body BY THE CROSS"* (Eph. 2:16).

Those who have difficulty seeing how the new covenant affects us should carefully read Rom. 3:19 and reflect how the old covenant, though made only with Israel, nevertheless *condemns* all the world. And was not the new covenant given to displace the old? (Heb. 10:9).

The old covenant condemns us, not because it was made with us, but simply because it proclaims the standards of God's holiness, "without which no man shall see the Lord" (Heb. 12:14). It was made with Israel because the Gentiles "did not like to retain God in their knowledge" and He had given them up (Rom. 1:28).

Likewise the new covenant speaks redemption to us, not because it was made with us, but because the blood of the new covenant met the claims of the old, that the old might be taken out of the way.

Should some reader still have difficulty understanding how the new covenant can affect members of the Body of Christ, he should bear in mind the simple *fact* that what was promised to Israel under the new covenant, *we have received* by grace through the shed blood of Christ.

THE MINISTRATION OF
CONDEMNATION AND DEATH

Contrasting the new covenant with the old, the Apostle points out that "the letter" with its requirements and penalties, "killeth." Therefore the dispensation of the law is called *"the ministration of condemnation"* and *"the ministration of death"* (II Cor. 3:7,9).

The ministration of the law began in a blaze of glory. Mount Sinai was "altogether on a smoke...as the smoke of a furnace." There were thunderings and lightnings and an earthquake. There was the sound of a trumpet, exceeding loud. There was the glorious Shekinah cloud in which God Himself appeared and "spake all these words" (Ex. 19:9—20:1).

But ere Moses had even come down from the mount

with the tables of stone, the people were breaking the very first commandment, dancing like heathen about a golden calf.

From here on the ministration of the law took on another aspect. Judgment had to be pronounced and penalties inflicted. Nor could any escape its just sentence of condemnation and death. What had begun in glory now led only to gloom, "because *the law worketh wrath*" (Rom. 4:15).

" . . .for it is written: Cursed is every one that continueth not in all the things which are written in the book of the law to do them" (Gal. 3:10).

THE MINISTRATION OF RIGHTEOUSNESS AND LIFE

But there can be no gloom associated with the administration of the new covenant, says the Apostle, for under it righteousness and life are ministered to all who will receive them by faith. And this because the claims of the old covenant were fully met by Christ at Calvary. Thus the ministration of the new covenant outshines that of the old in every respect.

"But if the ministration of death, written and engraven in stones, was glorious . . . .

"How shall not the ministration of the Spirit be rather glorious?

"For if the ministration of condemnation be glory, much more doth the ministration of righteousness exceed in glory.

"For even that which was made glorious had no glory in this respect, by reason of the glory that excelleth.

"For if that which is done away was glorious, much more that which remaineth is glorious" (II Cor. 3:7-11).

94

What emotions must have filled the heart of Paul as he was first sent, by the grace of God, to minister righteousness and life to men cursed by sin! It was a foretaste of what Israel will one day receive by promise, but all the more remarkable because ministered in "this present evil age," entirely apart from the promises. Surely, *"where sin abounded, grace did much more abound."*

God still requires *perfect* righteousness, to be sure. His holy standards have by no means been lowered. But He also *provides* righteousness in Christ and His servants minister it to those who will receive it by faith. How it should thrill our hearts to realize that this wonderful ministry has also been committed to us! Read again the wonderful proclamation, and rejoice:

"But now the righteousness of God without the law is manifested, being witnessed by the law and the prophets;

"Even the righteousness of God which is by faith [fidelity] of Jesus Christ unto all and upon all them that believe; for there is no difference;

"For all have sinned, and come short of the glory of God;

"Being justified freely by His grace through the redemption that is in Christ Jesus.

"Whom God hath set forth . . . . to declare His righteousness . . . .

"To declare, I say, at this time His righteousness; that He might be just, and the justifier of him which believeth in Jesus" (Rom. 3:21-26).

"But to him that worketh not, but believeth on Him that justifieth the ungodly, his faith is counted for righteousness" (Rom. 4:5).

"Therefore being justified by faith, we have peace with God through our Lord Jesus Christ" (Rom. 5:1).

This, of course, is a judicial matter. Christ's righteousness is *counted* as ours. Our faith is *counted* for righteousness. Nothing is held against us on the books, so to speak, and this is of primary importance. But, as we have seen, God does even more than this for us. He imparts *life* by His Spirit, thus enabling us to do His will.

"For the law of the Spirit [i.e.] life in Christ Jesus, hath made me free from the law of sin and death" (Rom. 8:2).

Thank God for the law of the Spirit! As surely as God's Word from Sinai was a law, a fixed rule; as surely as sin works in our members; as surely as sin brings death, [2] so surely it is a "law," a fixed, inexorable rule, that "he that hath the Son hath *life*." It is *never* otherwise. The Spirit imparts life to every believer in Christ. And it is only this quickening power of the Spirit that enables us to live pleasing to God. In Rom. 8:11,12 the Apostle says:

"But if the Spirit of Him that raised up Jesus from the dead dwell in you, He that raised up Christ from the dead shall also quicken your mortal [3] bodies by His Spirit that dwelleth in you.

"Therefore, brethren, we are debtors, not to the flesh, to live after the flesh."

Thus every time we meet at the Lord's table to "remember" and "show forth" His death, we praise Him—or should praise Him—that the blood of the new

---

2. See the "laws" of Rom. 7:21-23.

3. Note: "Your *mortal* bodies," not "your *dead* bodies." This has to do with experiencing the resurrection life of Christ *now*.

covenant availed also for us and ministers to us both righteousness and life. The fact that none of this was *promised* to us makes this time of communion so much more blessed, for here we gather together as those who share in the blood and the merits of Christ wholly *by grace!*

Chapter XII

Our Answer
To Dispensational Arguments
Against the Celebration
of the Lord's Supper

Through the years we have received many letters suggesting that if we hold that water baptism has no place in God's program for our day, we should logically eliminate the Lord's Supper too. Interestingly, such letters have come from *both* traditional denomination-alists *and* extreme dispensationalists; *both* those who believe that the Church of today began at Pentecost *and* those who teach that it did not begin until or after Acts 28. The only difference has been that the former group believe we should practice *both* water baptism and the Lord's Supper, while the latter believe we should practice neither.

But here our "Acts 28" friends have joined our "Acts 2" friends in a wholly unscriptural assumption: that water baptism and the Lord's Supper belong together in God's program. This is *pure unfounded tradition*, and it is strange that even extreme dispensationalists should fall for it.

The *fact* is that water baptism and the Lord's Supper are *not* linked together in the Scriptures. Indeed, there are definite distinctions and even contrasts between the two, as we have pointed out in a booklet on this subject. [1]

DISTINCTIONS BETWEEN BAPTISM AND THE LORD'S SUPPER

Water baptism was an *Old Testament ordinance.*

The Lord's Supper is a *New Testament celebration.*

Water baptism, like all ordinances, was *"imposed."*

The Lord's Supper was *never* imposed.

Water baptism was *required for salvation.*

The Lord's Supper, never!

Water baptism was associated with our Lord's *manifestation* to Israel.

The Lord's Supper (in its present form) is associated with our Lord's *rejection* and *absence.*

Water baptism denoted an *un*finished work. [2] It was but a *symbol* of the cleansing which only Christ could effect.

The Lord's Supper celebrates the *finished work* of Christ.

Water baptism was a *single* act.

The Lord's Supper is celebrated *again and again.*

Water baptism was not included in Paul's special commission.

---

1. Here we re-publish some of the arguments presented in our booklet *The Lord's Supper, Its Place in God's Program For Today.*

2. Remember, it was Paul who first proclaimed the *finished* work of Christ.

The Lord's Supper was included in Paul's special commission.

WATER BAPTISM AN
OLD TESTAMENT ORDINANCE

Those who suppose that the New Testament begins at Matt. 1:1 will no doubt be amazed when we declare that water baptism was an Old Testament ordinance. Nevertheless we insist upon it as a simple fact.

The Old Testament, or Covenant, was taken away *by* the cross (Col. 2:14) but not, historically, at the time of the crucifixion. After His resurrection our Lord did not immediately reveal to the disciples that the Law had been dealt with on the cross. "All filled with the Holy Spirit," they still remained under the Law as the Book of Acts so clearly indicates. Peter at Pentecost did not preach: "But now the righteousness of God without the Law is manifested." The time for this had not yet come.

All that had been accomplished at the cross was not revealed until *"due time,"* through the Apostle Paul. It is not until he appears upon the scene that we hear such declarations as the following:

"But now the righteousness of God without the law is manifested, being witnessed by the law and the prophets" (Rom. 3:21).

"Being justified freely by His grace through the redemption that is in Christ Jesus:

"Whom God hath set forth to be a propitiation, through faith in His blood, to declare His righteousness for the remission of sins that are past, through the forbearance of God;

"To declare, I say, at this time, His righteousness: that He

100

might be just and the justifier of him which believeth in Jesus" (Rom. 3:24-26).

"For there is one God, and one Mediator between God and men, the man Christ Jesus;

"Who gave Himself a ransom for all, to be testified in due time.

"Whereunto I am ordained a preacher, and an apostle, (I speak the truth in Christ and lie not;) a teacher of the Gentiles in faith and verity" (I Tim. 2:5-7).

"But before faith came, we were kept under the law, shut up unto the faith which should afterwards be revealed" (Gal. 3:23).

So it was some time after the cross that the full accomplishments of our Lord's finished work were proclaimed and the Law was *historically* done away.

Water baptism, even under the "great commission," was commanded before this "due time" had come, before either the sin of man or the grace of God had been fully demonstrated. It was commanded while the kingdom promises were still held out to Israel and God offered to send the risen Christ back to earth to sit on David's throne if the favored nation would but repent (See Acts 2:29-31; 3:19,20).

But the baptism of repentance, the same baptism which Peter proclaimed at Pentecost (Acts 2:38) was *instituted* even *before* the cross by John the Baptist, who lived and died under the Old Covenant, *not* the New, as is commonly supposed.

And the rite of baptism goes back even farther than this, for under Moses those who ministered in the priest's office were to be baptized, or washed, with

101

water (Ex. 29:1,4). [3] And since Israel was to become "a *kingdom of priests*, and an holy *nation*" (Ex. 19:5,6, cf. Isa. 61:6), John baptized all who would repent in connection with his proclamation that the kingdom was "at hand."

This is why we find water baptism associated with the Messiahship of Christ under John the Baptist, who said:

"And I knew Him not, but that He should be made manifest to Israel. Therefore am I come baptizing with water" (John 1:31).

And this is why we find water baptism practiced during the Acts period, while God was still stretching forth His hands in mercy to Israel.

Water baptism, then, was distinctly an *Old Testament* ordinance. This is not so with regard to the Lord's Supper.

THE LORD'S SUPPER
A NEW TESTAMENT CELEBRATION

It is disappointing to find some well-meaning extremists calling the Lord's Supper the Passover.

Surely Luke 22:14-20 proves conclusively that *after* the observance of the Passover, our Lord instituted a *"remembrance"* of His death.

When Paul recounts what our Lord did and said at the Lord's Supper he mentions only bread and wine, while at the Passover there was certainly much more than this.

---

3. It should be carefully noted that the Old Testament washings, whether of people or things, are called *baptisms* (Gr., *baptismos*) (Mark 7:3-8; Heb. 6:2; 9:10).

The Passover, like water baptism, was an Old Testament ordinance, but the Lord's Supper is as distinctly associated with the *New* Testament, or Covenant.

"For this is My blood of the new testament . . ." (Matt. 26:28).

The Passover, like water baptism, spoke of an *un*-finished work, for if water cannot wash away sin, neither can the blood of bulls and goats take away sins (Heb. 10:4). Both were *shadows* of the redeeming work of Christ.

Because so many stumble over the fact that water baptism was practiced even *after* the cross, we repeat that the full results of Calvary were not manifested until "due time," through the Apostle Paul. Blood sacrifices, circumcision, the sabbaths and feast days likewise spoke of an *un*finished work, yet these were all observed after the cross—*by the Spirit-filled disciples.* This is simply because the time for the unfolding of God's secret purpose and the gospel of the grace of God was not ripe until God raised up that *other* apostle, Paul. Indeed, even then its unfolding and the passing away of the old order were gradual matters.

BUT—whereas the Passover and water baptism were Old Testament ordinances, the Lord's Supper is distinctly a New Testament *celebration.* The celebration of the Lord's death should never be classed with the ordinances, not even with the ordinance of baptism, for while water baptism spoke of an *un*finished work, the Lord's Supper is clearly a *celebration* of the *finished* work of Christ.

103

At least three times the Lord's Supper is stated to be *"in remembrance"* of Christ and His redemptive work.

Chapter XIII

Ritual and Reality

ARGUMENTS FROM REASON AND EMOTION

RITUAL AND HUMAN BEHAVIOR

One of our readers has written us regarding the adverse impact of religious ritual upon human behavior, and feels that this is an argument against present-day observance of the Lord's Supper.

We agree indeed that Rome and the heathen world have lowered moral and spiritual standards by *substituting* rituals for reality. They have placed their dependence upon so-called meritorious works to save them, rather than relying wholly on the *finished* work of Christ, and this has in general had an adverse impact on their conduct.

But is it quite correct to say that ritual, *in itself*, has this effect upon human behavior? Surely, in Old Testament times it would have been unbelief and disobedience *not* to observe the rituals which God had commanded. The most godly and spiritual believers of that day were those who were, like David, most careful about fulfilling such requirements, even though they understood that these rituals, *in themselves*, had no saving value. According to Deuteronomy it was sincere observance of these things that brought God's blessing, while defection from them always resulted in a lowering of moral and spiritual standards (Cf. Neh. 8 and note especially Vers. 14-18).

Does the reader object that these are not "Old Testament times"? True enough, but our point is simply that ritual *in itself* does not necessarily have an adverse effect upon human behavior. The offerings and sacrifices of Old Testament times did not have an adverse effect upon true and sincere believers—and this would be the more true where *celebrations* were concerned.

We do agree, of course, that the observance of so-called meritorious rituals *in this dispensation of grace* must necessarily have an adverse impact upon those who practice them, for this constitutes a rejection of God's revealed truth and a denial of the *finished* work of Christ. This is so where any ritual is felt to be meritorious even in some small degree, or was required for acceptance with God when Scripturally in order.

Here is where water baptism and the Lord's Supper fall into widely differing categories.

Water baptism was, when in order, required for the remission of sins (See Mark 1:4; 16:15,16; Acts 2:38; 22:16, *et al*). Manifestly, then, to practice this rite now must cast reflections upon the *finished* work of Christ for salvation. Does some reader protest that *he* does not practice it for the remission of sins, but only as a beautiful picture of what Christ has done for him? Yet if I should offer a bleeding lamb in sacrifice and use this same argument, he would condemn me on the ground that *"Christ our Passover has been sacrificed for us."* Should not the present-day practice of water baptism, then, be condemned on the same ground? Does the reader further object that water baptism was practiced after Christ had died and risen again and therefore is compatible with the gospel of the grace of God? We reply that three of the four Scripture passages cited above prove that water baptism was required *for the remission of sins* after Christ had risen from the dead. This is simply because the significance of the cross was not clearly revealed until it was proclaimed by Paul in his "preaching of the cross." Read Peter's Pentecostal address carefully and note that he does *not* offer Christ's finished work as the remedy for sin, but makes the demand: *"Repent and be baptized every one of you in the name of Jesus Christ for the remission of sins"* (Acts 2:38).

The case is very different—in fact, the exact opposite—with regard to the Lord's Supper, for this was *never* required for the remission of sins, but on the contrary was said to be *a remembrance of the death of Christ* for the remission of sins (Matt. 26:28).

It follows from this that to observe the Lord's Supper for the remission of sins, as some denominations do, is an even greater denial of Scripture truth and a greater offense to God than to observe any other "meritorious" ceremony, for the Lord's Supper is a memorial of redemption *accomplished*.

From all this it should be observed how unscriptural it is to put baptism and the Lord's Supper in the same category. They were not instituted at the same time. They did not pass away at the same time, for the Lord's Supper, unlike water baptism, was carried over into the present economy. Again, water baptism was *required* for the remission of sins, while the Lord's Supper is a celebration of sins gloriously remitted. Furthermore Paul, the apostle of the Gentiles, declares

107

that he was *not* sent to baptize (I Cor. 1:17), while in the same epistle he says, with regard to the celebration of the Lord's Supper: *"I received of the Lord that which also I delivered unto you"* and *"as often as ye eat this bread, and drink this cup, ye do show the Lord's death till He come"* (I Cor. 11:23,26).

Another questioner writes: "Is the Lord so blind that He does not know our thoughts, but requires some kind of physical act from us so that He may understand us?" Our answer to this question is twofold:

DOESN'T GOD KNOW OUR HEARTS?

1. The Lord's Supper is not meant to help *Him* to understand or appreciate our worship, but rather to help *us* appreciate the stupendous fact that to lift us to a place in the heavenlies He had to become Man so that His body might be broken and His blood shed for us. This becomes abundantly clear as we read Paul's writings to the Corinthians on the subject.

2. The question itself is not pertinent. The truly pertinent question is simply: Do the Scriptures teach the celebration of the Lord's Supper in this present dispensation? The answer to this question is clearly in the affirmative. Paul had emphasized, in I Corinthians, the all-sufficiency of Christ's finished work to save, and in this same epistle he "delivers" the Lord's Supper as a memorial of that finished work.

"I NEVER FELT MOVED"

Another argument already considered against the celebration of the Lord's Supper is a purely emotional one. Again and again we have received letters from sincere believers who have argued against this practice because it seemed boring to them and left them cold, as it were. "I never felt moved at the Lord's table," writes one of these, and concludes that therefore it must not be in order for this dispensation!

Shall we then judge whether a practice is Scriptural or unscriptural by our emotional reaction to it? Shall we go by feeling rather than by faith; by the will of man rather than by the Word of God?

Many have testified that they were filled with joy and peace when they were baptized with water. Does this make the practice Scriptural for our day? Of course not, for many religious people of many faiths have testified to "blessing" received from observing the most unscriptural ceremonies.

Many do not feel moved at the Lord's table because its true meaning is not appreciated—sometimes even by those who administer it. Often it is "observed" as a solemn ordinance rather than as the glad celebration, the blessed memorial, it was meant to be.

The Scriptures are as much against the legalistic way in which many of the brethren observe the Lord's Supper as they are against the imposition of water baptism today. The Lord's Supper is not a mass. It is something infinitely more precious than that.

Scripture Passages
for
ONE HUNDRED HOMILIES
FOR THE COMMUNION SERVICE

*From the Upper Room
to Calvary*

INTRODUCTORY EXPLANATION

Generally the Communion Service is held at the close of a regular service at which the Word of God has been preached. Thus *another* preaching service hardly seems appropriate. Yet many pastors long for just the right thing to say at this time since the Communion Service is, of all services, *devotional* in character. It is a special service at which we remember with gratitude our Lord's suffering and death for us.

Thankfully, the record of the events of the few fleeting hours from the "upper room" through Calvary abounds with brief statements and phrases that yield much light and blessing as we meditate upon them. We have selected one hundred of these for brief homilies at the Lord's Table.

To pastors who may read this book, we suggest: Take any one of the following passages and, having read it in its context, simply *ponder* over it, *meditate* on it *prayerfully*, and blessed truths will come to mind which you will want to discuss at the Communion Service. Take, for example, No. 15: *"He brake it,"* and *think*. *"He* brake it"; *He* broke this symbol of His own body. Then compare this with John 10:17,18 (which will probably already have come to mind), and you will have plenty to talk about. Or take No. 18: "He took the cup and gave thanks." Just think, that cup contained the symbol of His life's blood, which was to be poured out within a few hours—and He *gave thanks!* As you think about it, Heb. 12:2 will doubtless readily come to mind, and again you will have plenty to talk about. Our hearts should overflow with such blessed truths. In fact, here we must add a word of caution: Don't make a long sermon of it, or weary hearers will *lose* the blessing. Just share your thoughts about it in a few simple words that will touch and bless the hearts of your hearers.

The author has used many of these Scripture passages for brief homilies at communion services and has often been touched as he has witnessed the blessings such simple thoughts have brought to the hearers.

May the following passages regarding our Lord's suffering and death bless the heart of many a pastor, and through him, the hearts of his hearers.

Scripture Passages For
ONE HUNDRED HOMILIES
FOR THE COMMUNION SERVICE

*From the Upper Room
to Calvary*

Section I
THE UPPER ROOM

1. The Passover Lamb .... Luke 22:1,2; I Cor. 5:7
2. My Time is At Hand .... Matt. 26:18
3. A Large Upper Room,
    Furnished and Prepared .... Mark 14:15
4. He Sat Down With the Twelve .... Matt. 26:20
5. He Loved Them Unto the End .... John 13:1
6. One of You Shall Betray Me .... Matt. 26:21
7. They Were Exceeding Sorrowful .... Matt. 26:22
8. Lord, Is It I? .... Matt. 26:22
9. One Whom Jesus Loved .... John 13:23
10. That Thou Doest, Do Quickly .... John 13:27
11. He Went Out, and It Was Night .... John 13:30
12. Thirty Pieces of Silver .... Matt. 26:14,15
13. The Same Night
    In Which He Was Betrayed .... I Cor. 11:23
14. Jesus Took Bread and Blessed It .... Matt. 26:26
15. He Brake It .... I Cor. 11:24
16. Broken For You .... I Cor. 11:24
17. Take, Eat, This is My Body .... Matt. 26:26
18. He Took the Cup,
    and Gave Thanks .... Matt. 26:27; Heb. 12:2

112

Section II
FROM THE UPPER ROOM
TO GETHSEMANE

Section III
THE BETRAYAL AND ARREST

Section IV
THE HEBREW AND ROMAN TRIALS

114

Section V
CALVARY

OTHER BOOKS BY THE SAME AUTHOR

Write for a Free Price List of All Our Literature

BEREAN BIBLE SOCIETY
PO Box 756
Germantown, WI 53022
(Metro Milwaukee)